ST. AUGUSTINE

THE FIRST
CATECHETICAL INSTRUCTION

[DE CATECHIZANDIS RUDIBUS]

Ancient Christian Writers

The Works of the Fathers in Translation

EDITED BY

JOHANNES QUASTEN, S. T. D.
*Professor of Ancient Church History
and Christian Archaeology*

JOSEPH C. PLUMPE, Ph. D.
*Professor of Patristic Greek
and Ecclesiastical Latin*

The Catholic University of America
Washington, D. C.

No. 2

ST. AUGUSTINE

THE FIRST CATECHETICAL INSTRUCTION

[De Catechizandis Rudibus]

TRANSLATED AND ANNOTATED

BY

THE REV. JOSEPH P. CHRISTOPHER, Ph. D.

Professor of Latin
Immaculate Conception Seminary
Darlington, New Jersey

NEWMAN PRESS

New York, N.Y./Ramsey, N.J.

Nihil Obstat:
>Johannes Quasten, S.T.D.
>*Censor Deputatus*

Imprimatur:
>Thomas J. Walsh, S.T.D., J.C.D.
>*Archiepiscopus Novarcensis*
>*die 11 Novembris 1946*

Library of Congress
Catalog Card Number: 78-62449

ISBN: 0-8091-0047-9

PUBLISHED BY PAULIST PRESS
Editorial Office: 1865 Broadway, New York, N.Y. 10023
Business Office: 545 Island Road, Ramsey, N.J. 07446

PRINTED AND BOUND IN THE UNITED STATES OF AMERICA

CONTENTS

ST. AUGUSTINE

THE FIRST
CATECHETICAL INSTRUCTION

Augustine, *Retractationes* 2. 14: There is also a book of ours on the first catechetical instruction; such is the actual title given it. In this book, where I have said: "Not even did the angel who with other spirits, his henchmen, forsook his obedience to God through pride and became the devil, do any hurt to God, but only to himself. For God knows how to make *souls* that forsake Him conform to the divine order," it would have been more consistent to say "*spirits* that forsake Him," since angels were spoken of. This book begins as follows: "You have asked me, brother Deogratias."

INTRODUCTION

The system of religious instruction obtaining in the early Church may have been inherited, at least in part, from either of the systems of oral instructions followed in the synagogue and in the pagan schools, or from both. The earliest form of catechetical instruction in the Church is represented by the instructions mentioned in the epistles of St. Paul; the next specimen would be probably the *Didache* (*ca.* 130). Such instruction reached its highest development in the catechetical school of Alexandria, though, strictly speaking, catechesis in the Alexandrian school meant rather a philosophical presentation of Christian dogma to meet the needs of cultured pagans and to refute heresy; it was, therefore, not so much a catechesis as an apology; just as the catechetical oration of St. Gregory of Nyssa was intended not for the catechumens but for catechists.

The Church required her converts to submit to four periods of instruction. In this system there was really only one class of catechumens.[1] These, who had acquired the right of being termed Christians, went through the longest period of catechesis and so also formed the largest class instructed. Candidates for admission to the catechumenate constituted another class, the *accedentes*, with whom we are here concerned. Those who had graduated from the catechumenate in virtue of the fact that their petition for admission to baptism had been approved, formed a third class, called *competentes* (*electi, illuminandi*); while the newly baptized, who continued to receive catechetical instruction during the octave of

3

Easter, constituted a fourth, the *neophyti*. Of Cyril's catechetical lectures eighteen were addressed to the *competentes*, five, to the *neophyti*. The first book of Ambrose's *De Abraham* is written for *catechumeni*, while his *De mysteriis* addresses itself to *neophyti*. Again, ten of the recently (1933) published catecheses of Theodore of Mopsuestia are for *competentes*, six, for *neophyti*. As a catechetical instruction for the *accedentes*, or candidates for admission to the catechumenate, the *De catechizandis rudibus* is the only treatise that has come down to us.

The class of *accedentes* was composed of pagans and heretics, the children of Christian parents receiving religious instructions at home.[2] Such prospective converts were also termed *rudes*, as they are termed in the title of the present treatise. The adjective *rudis* normally means "raw," "rough," "unpolished," "ignorant," "untaught"; but as a designation for one seeking admission to the catechumenate, it referred only to his being *untaught* in matters concerning the Christian religion which he wished to embrace. The term, in other words, has no reference whatever to the intellectual attainments and qualifications of the candidate. The *rudis* may be a rustic or he may be an educated man.[3]

When the candidate had given a satisfactory account of his motives for approaching Christianity, his preparation for admission to the catechumenate was given in a single instruction. In presenting it Augustine used the lecture method, interrupted occasionally and as the case seemed to require, by the auxiliary method of question-and-answer.[4] When the catechist had brought this instruction to a close, he asked the candidate whether he believed what he had heard. If the answer was in the affirmative, he was initiated into the catechumenate by the " sacraments " of the signing of the Cross, the imposition of hands, and the administration of salt.[5]

Augustine composed this treatise at the instance of Deogratias, a deacon friend of Carthage who, though a successful
catechist, was desirous of further guidance in the ministry of
catechizing. He was anxious to know especially with what
period his *narratio*—the exposition of Bible history—should
begin and how much it should include; and whether an
exhortatio should be added, or whether a brief statement of
the precepts governing the Christian manner of life would
suffice. It appears moreover that the zealous deacon was
apprehensive of growing stale in his instructions and felt that
he should seek advice and inspiration from his good friend,
the bishop of Hippo. The treatise with which Augustine
responded was written probably about the year 405.[6] It is
divided into two parts: the first, setting forth in fourteen
chapters the materials and methods of the instruction; the
second, containing two model catecheses, a longer (16-25)
and a shorter one (26 f.).

This treatise is therefore unique inasmuch as it embodies
both a manual for the catechist and a catechesis for the prospective catechumen. It is at once a contribution to the
subject-matter and the method of catechetics. Further, in all
catechetical treatises prior to Augustine (cf., e. g., the *Constitutiones Apostolorum* or Irenaeus's *Demonstratio praedicationis apostolicae*) the *narratio* was restricted to Bible history;
in the present treatise Augustine includes Church history
down to his own time. Moreover, in all catechetical treatises
before Augustine's time moral teaching was based on " the
doctrine of the two ways." [7] This is true even of the *Constitutiones Apostolorum* and the *Didascalia*, which though
venerating the Decalogue do not make it the norm of
Christian morality. Augustine is the first writer on catechetics
to point out that the Decalogue, as summed up in the two

great commandments of love of God and love of our neighbor, is the foundation of Christian morality.[8] Again, in addition to amplifying the *narratio* he outlined the following points in response to the deacon's query: 1. A brief apology for the dogma of the resurrection of the body; 2. an eschatology; 3. an ethical exhortation, which is the practical application of the *narratio*.

As for his contribution to the method of catechizing, Augustine was the first to appreciate the value of question and answer in studying the candidate and in sifting his motives for wishing to become a Christian. He likewise was the first to utilize for religious instruction many other sound principles of pedagogy and psychology, as, for example, not to confuse the candidate with too much matter, but to explain a little, clearly and thoroughly; to have but one central theme, the love of God; to give, as far as possible, individual instruction; to look to the candidate's bodily comfort; to adapt the instruction to the candidate's intelligence; to keep up interest, cultivate cheerfulness, and combat weariness.[9]

Looked at historically, this treatise, though one of Augustine's minor works, is important for further reasons. It is one of the first works of his maturity. In it he philosophizes on history and develops the idea of the two cities, which was later on to form the subject of his great work *De civitate Dei*. As a first textbook of catechetics this treatise is a worthy companion volume to the first textbook of homiletics, to be written some twenty years later when he completed the *De doctrina christiana*.[10] The *De catechizandis rudibus* gives a fairly detailed picture of church life immediately after the persecutions, furnishing interesting sidelights on the Manichaean, Donatist, and Pelagian heresies and controversies, and showing that even among Christians paganism, or at any rate, the pagan view of life, was not wholly destroyed. Further, it is of great help in studying manners and customs in the Roman Africa of the fifth century.

What sources did St. Augustine use in composing the *De catechizandis rudibus?* There are no direct references in this treatise to earlier works on catechetics. The general matter of catechesis could have been acquired from the *Didache*, the works of Origen (particularly the treatises *Contra Celsum* and *De principiis*), and from Tertullian and Ambrose. Among those who had written on the Decalogue before Augustine may be mentioned Lactantius in his *Epitome divinarum institutionum*, with which Augustine was familiar,[11] and Philo in *De Decalogo*. But though Augustine quotes Philo in his treatise *Contra Faustum* (12. 30), he most probably had never read his treatise on the Decalogue, being influenced against the work by Ambrose, who ignored it.[12] When on the subject of the resurrection of the body, Augustine employs the arguments and comparisons, and frequently the very words, of Minucius Felix and Tertullian. The two treatises, however, which resemble most the present work of St. Augustine are the *Constitutiones Apostolorum* and the *Demonstratio praedicationis apostolicae* of St. Irenaeus, written about the year 190 and the recovery of which in an Armenian translation constituted a major sensation among patrologists in our century. The study of very considerable resemblances of certain sections of Augustine's treatise to passages in the two older works [13] leads to the conclusion that all three compositions ultimately derive from an original, well-defined catechetical model.

The *De catechizandis rudibus* is moreover peculiarly interesting from the standpoint of the style in which it is written. Augustine was a master of several styles which he employed according to the nature of the work and the occasion. The style of this treatise is simple and correct, moving along clearly and vigorously; the arrangement of matter is logical and methodical. There are whole passages which for elegance, beauty, epigrammatic power, and unction can hardly be surpassed.[14] While it is true that the treatise, due to Augustine's practice of dictating,[15] gives some evidence of carelessness and haste in composition, it is equally true that in it there is no style for style's sake alone. In fact, Augustine here shows himself so conscious of his obligations to his hearers and readers that, as has been pointed out on the basis of syntactical and rhythmical studies made of the language he uses,[16] he employed two distinct styles in composing our treatise: one for the theoretical part addressed to the deacon and catechist Deogratias; the other, for the practical part to serve the catechizing of the prospective convert. The one medium of address, while simple and fairly unrhetorical, is still quite on the level of more cultured diction. In the other, in which Augustine discourses as a catechist, the language is adapted to the popular ear and comprehension, a policy followed by Augustine also in his sermons. But very obviously the master succeeded in wedding these mediums so skillfully, that only very recent research has established the fact of so fine a discrimination in composition.

Since St. Augustine composed this treatise on such sound principles of pedagogy and psychology, it is not surprising to find that upon it are based almost all subsequent works on catechetics. The monastic schools, which, beginning with the sixth century, gradually supplanted the pagan rhetorical schools, were greatly influenced by the educational principles of St. Augustine, as set forth particularly in De doctrina christiana and De catechizandis rudibus. Cassiodorus (ca.

490–ca. 583) in his important work *Institutiones divinarum et saecularium lectionum*, in which he makes monastic education to consist in a thorough training in rhetoric coupled with an equally thorough study of the Scriptures, follows very closely these two works. The *Etymologiae* of Isidore of Seville (ca. 550-636) which was the encyclopedia of the Middle Ages, was likewise based upon them. In Ireland the influence of Augustine on monastic education is well-known. In England, Bede and Alcuin, under whom the monastic schools reached their highest development, used *De catechizandis rudibus* and *De doctrina christiana* as textbooks. In Germany the *De institutione clericorum* of Hrabanus Maurus (ca. 784-856), Alcuin's most distinguished pupil, is but these two treatises worked over and adapted. The next great names in the chain of inheritance from Augustine are Petrarch, Erasmus, and Vives, all of whom were steeped in Augustine's theory of education. When after the invention of printing a number of catechisms began to flood Germany, George Wicelius in his *Catechismus Ecclesiae* (1535) was the first to write a catechism along the lines laid down by St. Augustine in his treatise. For France the names of Fleury, Pouget, and Bourgeaut may be mentioned as having written such catechisms. In 1830 Archbishop Augustine Gruber gave lectures on St. Augustine's *De catechizandis rudibus*, and in 1832 brought out a catechism based on it.[17] In our own time J. Eising has shown conclusively that the famous " Munich Method " of catechizing is modeled on this treatise.[18]

If we judge of a work by the influence it has exerted, then indeed must the *De catechizandis rudibus* be called a golden little book. Bishop William Turner, writing on St. Augustine in *The Catholic University Bulletin* 18 (1912) 20, says:

" His manual on how to teach Catechism to the unlettered does him more credit, we think, than all his learned works on philosophy and theology." Even in this treatise, small as it is, we may watch the master working in the maturity of genius; we may likewise understand why it is that only four names can be ranked with Augustine's in the influence they have exerted upon European thought and literature: Cicero, Augustine's master, upon whose writings European prose-style as a work of art is founded; Vergil, whom Augustine loved, the schoolbook of the Middle Ages; Quintilian, his teacher, upon whose *Institutiones oratoriae* the whole theory and practice of European education is based; and finally Jerome, his friend and fellow laborer, with the matter and form of whose Vulgate European literature is saturated.

✦   ✦   ✦

The present volume is an adaptation and revision of my larger work which appeared as Vol. 8 of The Catholic University of America Patristic Studies: *S. Aureli Augustini Hipponiensis episcopi de catechizandis rudibus liber unus. Translated with Introduction and Commentary* (Washington 1926). In this monograph I have used the Benedictine text of the late seventeenth century as reproduced by G. Krüger, *Augustin De catechizandis rudibus* (2nd ed., Tübingen 1909 [3d ed., 1934]). He departed from this text in four places only. I have followed him in two: 4. 8 *proposita* for *proposito*; 6. 10 *narrationis* for *rationis*. During the intervening decades a new text has not appeared in the Vienna *Corpus*. The translation has been improved in numerous instances. For this purpose I have also compared the variants published from a 12th century manuscript (Additional 14784, British Museum) by A. Souter: " Notes on the De Catechizandis

Rudibus," *Miscellanea Agostiniana* 2 (Rome 1931) 253-55; only two of these were adopted: 20. 34 *virga mare* for *virga* and 22. 39 *electus est* of the MSS. for *dictus est*. Souter's article sustains what he had observed earlier (*Speculum* 2 [1927] 215; note also his observations in *Journ. of Theol. Stud.* 28 [1927] 446), namely, that " it is improbable that much serious improvement can be made " on the Benedictine recension. The commentary has been recast and condensed very considerably to bring it into conformity with the purposes of the series, ANCIENT CHRISTIAN WRITERS. The philological especially has yielded to a greater insistence on the theological with all that the term embraces in the history of early Christianity. A number of corrections have been made, for some of which I am indebted to reviewers of the earlier work. In other instances new notes have been added, and throughout notice has been taken of the literature that has appeared these past twenty years.[19]

Part One

THE THEORY OF CATECHESIS

(Chapters 1-15)

a) Introduction (Chapters 1-2):

CHAPTER 1

St. Augustine writes in answer to Deogratias, a deacon of Carthage, who has asked what should be the subject matter and what the method in catechizing candidates.

You have asked me,[1] brother Deogratias,[2] to write something to you[3] on the instructing of candidates for the catechumenate[4] that may be of use to you. For you tell me that at Carthage,[5] where you are a deacon,[6] those who are to be grounded in the rudiments of the Christian faith are often brought to you, because you are supposed to possess great ability in catechizing,[7] by reason both of your thorough training in the faith[8] and the charm of your style: but that you are almost always perplexed to discover how suitably to present that truth, the belief in which makes us Christians; where to begin the narration,[9] to what point it should be brought down, and whether at the close of the narration an exhortation should be added, or precepts[10] only, in the observance of which he to whom we are speaking may know that the Christian life and profession[11] are maintained. You have had, moreover, to acknowledge and complain that often, because you talked too long and with too little enthusiasm, it has befallen you to become commonplace and wearisome even to yourself, not to mention him whom you were trying to instruct by your discourse, and the others who were present as listeners; and so you have felt obliged earnestly to entreat me, by the affection I owe you, not to consider it troublesome, occupied though I am with other things, to set down for you something on this subject.

2. For my part, I am constrained not only by the love and service which I owe you as a friend, but also by that which I owe to Mother Church [12] as one of her children (if through my assistance, which by the bounty of our Lord I am able to render, the Lord likewise bids me help in any way those whom He has made my brethren), in no wise to refuse but rather to undertake the task with a ready and earnest will. For the more widely I desire the Lord's treasure to be distributed, the more am I bound when I perceive that the stewards, my fellow servants, find any difficulty in dispensing it, to do all that I can that they may be able to compass easily and readily what they diligently and earnestly desire.

CHAPTER 2

A disappointing experience: the inadequacy of language to express thought. But let the catechist take courage.

3. But as regards your reflections on your own case, I would not have you be disturbed because you have frequently seemed to yourself to be delivering a worthless and wearisome discourse. For it may very well be that it was not so regarded by him whom you were endeavoring to instruct, but because you were earnestly desiring to have something better for your hearers, on this account what you were saying did not seem worthy of others' ears. For my part, I am nearly always dissatisfied with my discourse. For I am desirous of something better, which I often inwardly enjoy before I begin to unfold my thought in spoken words; but when I find that my powers of expression come short of my knowledge of the subject, I am sorely disappointed that my tongue has not been able to answer the demands of my mind. For I desire my hearer to understand all that I understand; and I feel that I am not speaking in such a manner as to effect that. This is so chiefly because intuition floods the mind, as it were, with a sudden flash of light, while the expression of it in speech is a slow, drawn-out, and far different process, and while speech is being formed, intellectual apprehension has already hidden itself in its secret recesses; nevertheless, because it has stamped in a wonderful way certain imprints upon the memory, these endure for the length of time it takes to pronounce the words; and from these imprints we construct those audible symbols which are called language, whether it be Latin, or Greek, or Hebrew, or any other tongue, whether these symbols exist in the mind or are actually uttered by the voice, though these marks are neither Latin, nor Greek, nor Hebrew, nor peculiar to any other race, but are produced in the mind as is the expression of the face in the body. For instance, anger is designated by one word in Latin, by another in Greek, and by others again in the various other tongues; but the expression on the face of an angry man is neither Latin nor Greek. Thus it is that not all nations understand when a man says: *Iratus sum*, but Latins only; but if the feeling present in his mind as it kindles to white heat comes out upon his features and gives him a

certain look, all who see him understand that he is angry.
But again, it is not in our power to bring forth those imprints
which intellectual apprehension stamps upon the memory
and, as it were, submit them by the sound of our voice to
the perception of those listening, in any way parallel to the
open and evident expression of the face. For the former are
within, in the mind; but the latter is without, in the body.
And, therefore, we may infer how much the sound of our
voice differs from that instantaneous flash of intellectual
apprehension, seeing that it does not resemble even the
memory-impression. Often, moreover, burning with a desire
to help our hearer, we wish to express ourselves in exact
accord with our understanding of the matter at that moment
but find that, owing to the very strain of our mental effort,
we cannot speak; and then because of our failure we are
vexed and, as though we were having our pains for naught,
we wilt from weariness; and, as the result of this very weariness, our discourse itself becomes more dull even than it was
at the moment when it first caused listlessness.

4. But often the eagerness of those who desire to hear
me shows me that my discourse is not so dull as it seems to
me. From the enjoyment, too, which they manifest I gather
that they receive some benefit from it. And so I take great
pains not to fail in offering this service, in which I see what
is offered so well received by them. In like manner you also,
from the very fact that those who are to be instructed in the
faith are so often brought to you, ought to be convinced that
your discourse is not so unsatisfactory to others as to yourself,
and you ought not to account your efforts fruitless simply
because you do not express so clearly as you wish the things
which you perceive; since perhaps you cannot even perceive
them as you desire. For who in this life sees except as *in a*

dark manner and through a glass? [13] And not even love itself
is so mighty as to rend asunder the gross darkness of the
flesh [14] and pierce to that eternal clearness [15] from which even
transitory things derive their radiance, such as it is. But
because the good are advancing from day to day toward the
vision of that day which knows neither revolution of the
heavens nor onset of night,[16] that day *that eye hath not seen,
nor ear heard, neither hath it entered into the heart of man,*[17]
there is no greater reason why our discourse becomes cheap-
ened in our eyes when teaching candidates than that we
like to discern the truth in an unusual way but weary of
expressing it in the usual manner. Indeed, people listen to
us with much greater pleasure when we ourselves take
pleasure in this same work of instruction. The thread of our
discourse is affected by the very joy that we ourselves experience, and as a consequence is delivered more easily and
received more gratefully. Accordingly, it is no hard task to
give directions in regard to those truths which are instilled
as articles of faith—where the narration should be begun and
where ended; [18] and again, how it should be varied, so as to
be shorter at one time, longer at another, and yet at all times
absolutely complete, and when the shorter and when the
longer form should be used. But our chief concern is what
means we should adopt to ensure that the catechizer enjoys
his work; for the more he is able to do so, the more agreeable
will he prove. And a directive indeed for this is ready at
hand. For if in the case of material wealth *God loves a
cheerful giver,*[19] how much more in that of spiritual? But
that the catechist may have this cheerfulness in the hour of
need depends on the mercy of Him who has given these commandments. Therefore, we shall discuss, as God shall suggest
to us,[20] first the method to be followed in the narration—

as I understand is your desire; then the duty of admonition and exhortation,[21] and lastly the means by which the cheerfulness in question is to be secured.

b) The Narration (Chapters 3-6):

CHAPTER 3

The subject matter of the instruction: a summary treatment of the Old Testament history in which the various events are made to converge upon the coming of Christ.

5. The narration is complete when the beginner is first instructed from the text: *In the beginning God created heaven and earth,* down to the present period of Church history.[22] That does not mean, however, that we ought to repeat verbatim the whole of the Pentateuch,[23] and all the books of Judges and Kingdoms [24] and Esdras, and the entire Gospel [25] and the Acts of the Apostles (if we have learned them by heart), or relate in our own words all that is contained in these books, and thus develop and explain them; for which neither time serves nor any need calls. But we ought to present all the matter in a general and comprehensive summary, choosing certain of the more remarkable facts that are heard with greater pleasure and constitute the cardinal points in history; [26] these we ought not to present as a parchment rolled up [27] and at once snatch them out of sight, but we ought by dwelling somewhat upon them to untie, so to speak, and spread them out to view, and offer them to the minds of our hearers to examine and admire. But the remaining details we should weave into our narrative in a rapid survey. In this way not only are the points which we desire

most to emphasize brought into greater prominence by keeping the others in the background, but also he whose interest
we are anxious to stimulate by the narration does not reach
them with a mind already exhausted, and we avoid confusing
the memory of him whom we ought to instruct by our
teaching.

6. In all things, indeed, it not only behooves us to keep
in view the goal of the precept, which is *charity from a pure
heart, and a good conscience, and an unfeigned faith* [28]—a
standard to which we should make all that we say refer; but
towards it we should also move and direct the attention of.
him for whose instruction we are speaking. And, in truth,
for no other reason were all the things that we read in the
Holy Scriptures written before our Lord's coming than to
announce His coming and to prefigure the Church to be, that
is to say, the people of God throughout all nations, which
Church is His body,[29] in which are included and numbered
all the just who lived in this world even before His coming
and who believed that He would come as we believe that He
has come.[30] For as Jacob, when he was being born, put forth
first from the womb his hand, with which he also held the
foot of his brother who was being born before him, his head,
of course, followed next, and lastly of necessity the remaining
members of his body; yet, for all that, in dignity and power
the head comes not only before those members which followed it, but even before the hand which in the process of
birth outstripped it; and although not in the time of its appearance, yet in the order of nature it is prior. So too our Lord
Jesus Christ, *who is over all, God blessed forever,*[31] even
before He appeared [32] in the flesh and in a sense came forth
from the womb of His secret dwelling before the eyes of men
as *Mediator between God and men,*[33] sent before Him in the

persons of the holy Patriarchs and Prophets some part of His body,[34] with which as with a hand He foretokened His future birth, and also in the bonds of the law, as by five fingers, seized by the heel and overthrew the people who went before Him in pride. For through five epochs His future coming ceased not to be foretold and prophesied, and in keeping with this, he through whom the law was given [35] wrote five books; and that proud people being carnal-minded, and seeking to establish their own justification,[36] were not filled with bless- ing from the open hand of Christ, but were shut out from it by that hand clenched and closed, and so their. feet were bound and *they fell, but we are risen, and are set upright.*[37]

Although, therefore, as I have said, the Lord Christ sent forth before Him a part of His body in the persons of the just who preceded Him in the time of their birth, nevertheless *He is Himself the head of His body, the Church,*[38] and by believing in Him [39] whom they foreshadowed all of them remained attached to that same body of which He is the head. For they were not separated from Him by being His pre- cursors, but rather were they joined to Him by their obedience to His will. For although the hand may be put forth before the head, yet its connection with the body is below the head. Therefore *all things that were written beforehand were written for our learning and were lessons for us, and by way of lesson happened one after another to them. Moreover, they were written for our sakes unto whom the consummation of the ages has reached.*[40]

CHAPTER 4

The chief reason for Christ's coming was to manifest and to teach God's love for us. Here the catechist should find the focal point of his instruction.

7. Moreover, what greater reason could there be for the Lord's coming than that God might manifest [41] His love [42] for us and ardently recommend it; *because when as yet we were enemies, Christ died for us?* [43] And for this reason, that, inasmuch as love is the *end of the commandment* and the *fulfillment of the law,* [44] we also may love one another, and even as *He laid down His life for us, so we also may lay down our life for the brethren.* [45] And with regard to God Himself, *inasmuch as He first loved us* [46] and *spared not His only Son, but delivered Him up for us all,* [47] even if at first we found it irksome to love Him, now at least, it should not prove irksome to return that love. [48] For there is nothing that invites love more than to be beforehand in loving: and that heart is overhard which, even though it were unwilling to bestow love, would be unwilling to return it. But if we see that even in the case of sinful and base attachments those who desire to be loved in return make it their one concern to disclose and display by all the tokens in their power how much they love; if they also strive to counterfeit genuine affection in order that they may, in some measure, claim a return of love from the heart which they are designing to ensnare; if, again, their own passions are the more inflamed when they perceive that the hearts which they are eager to win are also moved now by the same fire; if then, I say, both the hitherto callous heart is aroused when it is sensible of being loved, and the heart which was already aflame is the more inflamed the

moment it learns that it is loved in return, it is obvious that
there is no greater reason either for the birth or growth of
love than when one, who as yet does not love, perceives that
he is loved, or when he who loves already hopes either that
he may yet be loved in return, or actually has proof that he
is loved. And if this holds good even in the case of base
passions, how much more so in friendship? For what else
do we have to be on our guard against in an offense against
friendship than that our friend should think either that we
do not love him, or that we love him less than he loves us?
And if he believes this, he will be cooler in that love which
men enjoy by the exchange of intimacy; and if he is not so
weak that this offense causes him to grow cold in his affection
altogether, he yet restricts himself to that form of affection
which has as its object not enjoyment but utility.

But again, it is worth while to observe how, although even
those that are superior desire to be loved by those that are
inferior and are pleased by the eager deference these give
them—and the more they become sensible of this affection
the more they love them—yet, with how much love is one
who is inferior fired when he discovers that he is loved by
him who is superior. For love is more welcome when it is
not burnt up with the drought of want, but issues forth
from the overflowing stream of beneficence. For the former
springs from misery, the latter from commiseration.[49] And,
furthermore, if the inferior person has been despairing that
even he could be loved by the superior one, he will now be
unspeakably moved to love if the superior one deigns [50] of his
own accord to show him how much he loves one who could
by no means venture to promise himself so great a blessing.
But what could be higher than God when He judges, and
what more hopeless than man when he sins?—than man who

had so much the more submitted himself to the custody and
dominion of insolent powers which cannot make him blessed,
as he had the more despaired of the possibility of becoming
the care of that power which wills not to be exalted in
wickedness but is exalted in goodness?

8. If, therefore, Christ came chiefly for this reason that
man might learn how much God loves him, and might learn
this to the end that he might begin to glow with love of Him
by whom he was first loved, and so might love his neighbor
at the bidding and after the example of Him who made Himself man's neighbor by loving him, when instead of being His
neighbor he was wandering far from Him; if, moreover, all
divine Scripture that was written before was written to fore-
tell the coming of the Lord, and if whatever has since been
committed to writing and established by divine authority tells
of Christ and counsels love, then it is evident that on these
two commandments of the love of God and the love of our
neighbor depend not merely the whole law and the Prophets
(which at the time when the Lord uttered these precepts
were as yet the only Holy Scripture),[51] but also all the inspired
books that have been written at a later period for our welfare
and handed down to us.[52] Therefore, in the Old Testament
the New is concealed, and in the New the Old is revealed.[53]
In keeping with that concealment, carnal men, understanding
only carnally,[54] both then were, and now are, made subject
to the fear of punishment. But in keeping with this revelation spiritual men, understanding spiritually [55] (both those
of former times to whom, when they devoutly knocked, hidden things were revealed, and those of the present time, who
do not seek in pride, lest even what is manifest should be
hidden from them), are made free by the bestowal of love.
Since therefore nothing is more opposed to love than envy,[56]

and the mother of envy is pride,[57] the same Lord Jesus Christ, God-Man, is at once a token of divine love towards us and an example among us of man's lowliness,[58] to the end that our swollen conceit, great as it is, may be healed by an even greater antidote.[59] For the misery of man's pride is great, but the commiseration of God's humility is greater.

With this love, then, set before you as an end to which you may refer all that you say, so give all your instructions that he to whom you speak by hearing may believe, and by believing may hope, and by hoping may love.[60]

CHAPTER 5

The candidate should be questioned as to his motives in desiring to become a Christian.

9. Moreover, love must be built up out of that very sternness of God, which makes man's heart quail with a most salutary fear, so that man, rejoicing to find himself loved by Him whom he fears, may make bold to love Him in return, and at the same time may shrink from offending His love towards him, even if he could do so with impunity. For very rarely, nay, never, does it happen that any one comes to us with the desire to become a Christian, who has not been smitten with some fear of God.[61] For if he wishes to become a Christian in the hope of deriving some benefit from men whom he thinks he could not otherwise please, or to escape some injury at the hands of men whose displeasure or enmity he dreads, he in reality does not wish to become a Christian so much as he wishes to feign being one. For faith consists not in a body bending but in a mind believing. But undoubtedly the mercy of God is often present through the ministry of the catechist, so that a man impressed by the discourse now wishes to become in reality what he had decided to feign. And when he does begin to desire this let us assume that now at least he has come in earnest. True, it is hidden from us when it is that one whom we now see present in the body does really come in spirit; nevertheless, we should deal with him in such a manner that he may conceive this desire even though it does not as yet exist. For none of our labor is wasted, since if the desire is there, it is in any case strengthened by such dealing on our part, although we may be ignorant of the time or of the hour at which it began. It is well, certainly, to be informed, if possible, beforehand by those who know him of his state of mind and of the causes that have induced him [62] to come and embrace religion. But if there be no one else from whom we may learn this, we must question the candidate himself so that from his answers we may draw an opening for our instruction. But if he has come with a counterfeit motive, desirous only of temporal advantages, or thinking to escape some loss, he will, of course, lie. Yet you must derive your beginning from the very lie he tells. You must not do this, however, with the intention of unmasking his false pretense, as though sure of it; but if he says that he came with such an intention as is really praiseworthy, whether he be speaking the truth or not, we should nevertheless so approve and praise such an intention as that with which, according to his own reply, he came, as to make him take delight in being actually such as he desires to seem. But if, on the other hand, he says anything other than what ought to be in the mind of one who is about to receive first instructions in the Christian faith, then both by chiding him indulgently and gently,[63] as you would an uninstructed and ignorant person, and by pointing

out and praising the true goal of Christian teaching briefly
and impressively, so as neither to encroach on the time
allotted for the narration which is to follow, nor to venture to
impose that teaching upon a mind not previously prepared
for it, you may cause him to wish what, either through
ignorance or pretense, he had not heretofore wished.

CHAPTER 6

The instruction should begin with a narration of God's
dealings with man from the creation of the world down to
the present period of Church history; they should all be
referred to love as their final cause.

10. But if peradventure he answers that his becoming a
Christian is the result of a warning or dread inspired from
on high, he affords us a most happy opportunity for an opening on God's great care for us. We should direct his thoughts
from the guidance of wonders or dreams of this kind to the
more solid path and the more trustworthy oracles of the
Scriptures; [64] so that he may also understand how mercifully
that warning was vouchsafed him before he applied himself
to the Holy Scriptures.[65] And we should by all means point
out to him that the Lord Himself would not be warning or
constraining him to become a Christian and a member of
the Church, or training him by such signs or revelations, if
He had not wished him, for his greater safety and security, to
walk in the way already provided in the Holy Scriptures,
wherein he should not seek visible miracles but accustom
himself to hope for those that are invisible and should receive
warnings not when sleeping but when awake.[66] At this point
we should begin our narration, starting out from the fact

that God made all things very good,[67] and continuing, as we have said, down to the present period of Church history, in such a way as to account for and explain the causes and reasons [68] of each of the facts and events that we relate, and thereby refer them to that end of love from which in all our actions and words our eyes should never be turned away. For if, even as regards the fictitious tales of the poets, which were devised for the pleasure of minds that feed on trifles, the grammarians who are considered and called good [69] do nevertheless try to make them serve some useful purpose even though that very purpose be vain and greedy of worldly diet, how much more careful ought we to be lest the truths, which we relate without a well-ordered statement of their causes, should be accepted either for their own charm or even through a harmful curiosity in our hearers. Yet, at the same time, let us not set forth these causes in such a way as to abandon the course of the narration and permit our heart and tongue to stray into the more tangled mazes of controversy. But let the simple truth of the narration that we employ be like the gold which holds together in harmonious arrangement the jewels of an ornament without becoming itself unduly conspicuous.

c) THE EXHORTATION (CHAPTER 7):

CHAPTER 7

To the narration should be added the Church's doctrine on the last things of man. Temptation and scandals to be faced by the candidate during his catechumenate.

11. At the conclusion of the narration we should make known to him the hope in the resurrection, and with due regard for the capacity and powers of our hearer and the time at our disposal, combat by discussion the vain scoffings of unbelievers about the resurrection of the body,[70] and speak to him of the last judgment to come, with its goodness towards the good, its severity towards the wicked, its certainty in relation to all.[71] And after the punishments of the wicked have thus been recounted with loathing and horror, we should describe with eager longing the kingdom of the good and faithful, and that city in heaven with its joys.[72] Then, indeed, the natural infirmity of man should be armed and encouraged against trials and offenses, whether without or within the Church itself—without, as against pagans or Jews [73] or heretics; within, as against the chaff of the Lord's threshing floor.[74] This does not mean, however, that we are to argue against each class of perverse men, and refute all their crooked opinions by set arguments; but, as the shortness of time permits, we should show how this was so foretold, and point out in what way trials are profitable in training the faithful, and what a remedy there is in the example afforded by the forbearance of God, who has resolved to permit them to continue even unto the end.[75]

But, again, when the candidate is put on his guard against those depraved persons [76] who in mobs fill the churches in a bodily sense only, let also the precepts of a Christian, upright manner of life [77] be at the same time briefly and appropriately presented, that he may not be so easily led away by men who are drunkards, covetous, extortioners, gamblers, adulterers, fornicators, lovers of shows,[78] wearers of idolatrous charms, soothsayers, astrologers,[79] or diviners employing vain and unholy arts,[80] or any other such like persons; and because he sees many who are called Christians given to these practices and doing them and championing and recommending and promoting the adoption of them, he may not imagine that he can do such things and still go unpunished. For as to what is the end appointed for those who persist in such a life, and how they must be endured even in the Church itself, but from which they are destined to be separated in the end, we must instruct him fully by the evidences from the sacred books. We should also assure him that he will find many good Christians in the Church, most true citizens [81] of the heavenly Jerusalem, if he begins to be such himself. Finally, we must earnestly caution him against placing his hope in man, for it cannot easily be judged by man what man is truly good; [82] and tell him that even if it could easily be done, still the examples of good men are set before us not that we may be justified by them but that we may know that, if we imitate them, we also shall be justified by Him who justified them. [83] The result will be what we must especially commend, namely, that when he who is listening to us, or rather listening to God through us, [84] begins to make progress in morality and knowledge and to enter upon the way of Christ with eagerness he will not venture to ascribe the change either to us or to himself, but will love both himself and us, and any other friends he loves, in Him and for His sake, who loved him when he was yet an enemy, [85] in order that by justifying him He might make him a friend. And at this point of your instruction I do not think you need a monitor to tell you that when there are many calls on your own or your hearer's time you should be brief; and that, on the other hand, you should speak at greater length when you have more time at your disposal. For mere necessity will teach you this without anyone advising it.

d) The Treatment of Certain Candidates (Chapters 8-9):

CHAPTER 8

How to deal with the educated.

12. But there is one thing that obviously should not be passed over. I mean that if some one well-versed in liberal studies,[86] who has already made up his mind to be a Christian, comes to you to be catechized, and has come with the express intention of becoming a Christian, it can scarcely be that he has not already acquired a considerable knowledge of our Scriptures and literature, and thus already equipped has come now only to be made a partaker in the sacraments.[87] For such men are wont to investigate carefully every point beforehand, and not at the very hour in which they become Christians; beforehand also they are wont to make known the workings of their own minds to such others as they can and discuss them with them. With these, therefore, we must be brief and not dwell with annoying insistence upon things which they know, but, with discretion, touch lightly upon them. So that, for example, we may say that we believe they are already familiar with such and such a point; and in this way we pass rapidly in review all that has to be impressed upon the minds of the ignorant and unlearned; so that if there be any point that this educated man already knows, he may not have to listen to it as from a teacher;[88] and if, on the other hand, there be anything of which he is still ignorant, he may learn it while we are going over the points with which we assume he is already familiar. Moreover, it will certainly not be unprofitable to ask him what his motives for desiring to be a Christian are; so that if you see that he has been moved to that decision by books, whether the canonical [89] Scriptures or those of good writers, you may begin by saying something about these, recommending them according to their various merits, whether in respect of canonical authority or of the attention to detail and subtlety of the several interpreters; and in the canonical Scriptures praising above all their marvellous sublimity joined to most wholesome simplicity; [90] but in other works, a style of more sonorous and neatly-turned expression adapted, according to each writer's ability, to prouder, and therefore weaker, minds.

We must likewise, of course, draw him out to indicate clearly what writer he has read most, and by intimate familiarity with what books he has been won over to the desire of joining the Church. And when he has told us this, then if we are acquainted with these books, or at least if we know it to be the common belief of the Church that they were composed by some Catholic writer of note, let us gladly give them our approval. But if he has happened upon the volumes of some heretic and, unwittingly perhaps, has held and considers to be Catholic [91] what the true Church condemns, we must earnestly instruct him, setting before him the authority of the universal Church and that of other most learned men renowned for their disputations and writings concerning the truth of her teaching. And yet even those who have departed this life as Catholics, and have left to posterity some Christian literature, in certain passages of their works, either because they have not been understood, or else, as is the case with human infirmity, because they were not able by keenness of intellect to pierce the more hidden truths, and led astray from the truth by a semblance of truth, have served as an occasion to presumptuous and rash men to devise and beget some heresy. This is not to be wondered at since, starting

out from the canonical writings themselves in which everything has been expressed in the soundest and most rational
way, many have given birth to many pernicious dogmas,
thereby rending asunder the unity of our communion; [92]
and they have done this, not only by taking certain passages
in a sense different, either from that which the writer had
in mind or from that which is in accord with the truth itself
(for if that were all, who would not willingly forgive human
weakness when it showed itself ready to amend?),[93] but by
persistently championing their perverse and distorted opinions
with the bitterest vehemence and obstinate arrogance.

All these points we should treat in a discreet conference
with him who comes to join the fellowship of the Christian
people, not as an illiterate person, to use a common phrase,
but with all the education and culture gained from the works
of learned men, assuming on our part only so much of the
magisterial tone (that he may guard against the errors of
presumption) as his humility, which has brought him to us, is
now seen to permit of. But as for all else that is to be narrated
and expounded in accordance with the rules of sound doctrine, whether concerning faith, or morals, or temptations, it
should be treated in a rapid survey, as I have indicated above,
and directed to that more excellent way.[94]

CHAPTER 9

*How to deal with students from the schools of grammar
and rhetoric.*

13. There are also some who come from the ordinary
schools of grammar and rhetoric, whom you would neither dare
to class among the illiterate, nor yet among those very learned

men whose minds have been trained by the investigation of serious questions.[95] When, therefore, these men, who seem to surpass all other men in the art of speaking, come to be made Christians, we ought to convey to them more fully than to the illiterate an earnest warning to clothe themselves in Christian humility, and learn not to despise those whom they know as shunning more carefully faults of character than faults of diction;[96] and also that they should not even presume to compare with a pure heart the trained tongue which they had been wont even to prefer. But, most of all, they should be taught to listen to the divine Scriptures, so that solid diction may not seem mean to them merely because it is not pretentious,[97] and that they may not imagine that the words and deeds of men, of which we read in those books rolled up and concealed in fleshly coverings, are not to be unfolded and revealed so as to convey a meaning, but are to be taken literally. And as regards the actual value of a hidden meaning, from which these writings derive their name of mysteries, and the power of these concealed oracles[98] to sharpen the desire for truth and to shake off the torpor induced by surfeit, such men must have this shown them by actual experience, wherein something which failed to stir them when set plainly before them is brought to light by the unraveling of some allegory. For it is most useful for these men to know that the meaning is to be regarded as superior to words, just as the spirit is to be preferred to the body. And from this, too, it follows that they ought to prefer to hear true rather than eloquent discourses,[99] just as they ought to prefer to have wise rather than handsome friends.

Let them be assured, too, that there is no voice to reach the ears of God save the emotion of the heart.[100] Thus they will not smile contemptuously if they happen to observe that some ministers of the Church either fall into barbarisms and solecisms when calling upon Almighty God, or do not understand and badly punctuate words which they are pronouncing.[101] Not that such faults should not be corrected, so that the people may say " Amen " to what they plainly understand; but still they should be borne in a kindly spirit by those who have learned that just as in the law courts good speaking is effected by the voice, so in the church it is effected by prayer. Accordingly, though sometimes the language of the law courts may be called good speaking, it can never be called holy speaking. But with regard to the sacrament which they are about to receive, it is enough for the more intelligent to be told what that rite signifies, while with slower minds we should use somewhat more words and illustrations, that they may not consider lightly what they see.

e) The Disposition of the Catechist (Chapters 10-14):

CHAPTER 10

Various causes make the catechist feel antipathy for his task. The problem of adapting the discourse to the capacities and limitations of the audience.

14. At this point, perhaps, you are anxious to have some discourse as a model, so that I may point out to you by a concrete example how to do all these things that I have recommended. And this indeed I will do as far as by the Lord's help I am able. But I must first say something, as I promised, about acquiring that cheerfulness; for as touching the bare rules for developing your discourse in catechizing one who comes expressly to be made a Christian, I have already, in my opinion, sufficiently made good my promise. And surely I am not bound actually to do myself in this volume what I lay down as essential. If, therefore, I do so, it shall count as an extra measure of service on my part; but how can I add an extra measure before I have given the just measure?

Indeed the chief complaint that I have heard you make is that your discourse seemed to you to be a poor and mean thing when you were giving first instructions in the Christian faith.[102] But this, I know, results not so much from lack of things to say, with which I know you are sufficiently equipped and supplied, nor yet from lack of words themselves, but from weariness of mind. And that may spring either from the cause that I have mentioned, namely, that we are more charmed and arrested by that which we perceive in silence in our minds, and do not wish to be called off from it to babble of words which fall far short of reproducing it; or because, even when we like to speak, we like still better to hear or read things which have been better expressed, and which may be given by us without costing any care or anxiety on our part, than to frame hasty sentences offhand to convey truths to the understanding of another, in uncertainty [103] whether our words, as they come to us, are the ones we wanted, or whether, again, they are received by our hearers in a profitable way; or again, just because the subjects that the candidates have to be taught are now so thoroughly familiar to us and no longer necessary for our own progress, it irks us to return to them so often, and our mind, as having outgrown them, no longer moves with any pleasure in such well-trodden and, as it were, childish paths. Moreover, a hearer who remains unmoved makes the speaker weary; [104] [whether it be that he is actually not stirred by any emotion, or that he does not show by any gesture that he understands or that he approves what is said.] Not that it is a proper disposition in us to be eager for human praise, but because the things which we dispense are God's; and the more we love those to whom we speak, the more we desire them to enjoy what is proffered them for their salvation; so that if we do not succeed in this we are sore grieved and are crippled and broken in the course of the instruction itself as though we were expending our labor fruitlessly. Sometimes, too, when we are interrupted in some work which we are desirous of doing, and which we either liked to do or thought it more necessary to do, and are forced, either by the command of one whom we are unwilling to offend or by the unavoidable importunity of some persons, to catechize someone, we come with minds already upset to a work which requires great calmness, lamenting that we are not permitted to observe the order in our occupations that we desire to, and that we cannot possibly meet all the demands made upon us; and thus, as our discourse proceeds from our very distress, it is not so acceptable because, welling out of the parched soil of dejection, it has less richness.

Sometimes, again, grief takes possession of our hearts on account of some stumbling-block or other, and at that very time some one says to us, "Come, speak to this man; he wants to become a Christian." [105] For those who say it little know the hidden thought that is consuming us within. And if we may not discover to them our feelings we with rather ill grace undertake what they desire; and of course our instruction will be dull and unattractive, coming forth as it does through a channel of feeling that is seething and fuming. Out of so many possible causes, therefore, we must according to God's will seek remedies for the one, whichever it may be, that is actually beclouding the serenity of our minds; such remedies as may relieve that feeling of dejection, and help us to rejoice in fervor of spirit, and be glad in the peace of mind that the performance of a good work brings. *For God loveth a cheerful giver.*[106]

15. For if the cause of our sadness is that our hearer does not grasp our thought and so, descending after a manner from its lofty heights, we are obliged to spend time uttering one slow syllable after another which is on a far lower plane, and are at pains how that which is imbibed at one rapid draught of the mind may find utterance by long and devious paths through lips of flesh, and so, because it comes forth in a very different form, we are weary of speaking and wish to remain silent; then let us consider what has been vouchsafed to us beforehand by Him *who showed us an example, that we should follow His steps.*[107] For however widely our spoken word differs from the rapidity of our understanding, greater by far is the difference between mortal flesh and equality with God. And yet, *though He was in the* same *form, He emptied Himself, taking the form of a servant*, etc., *even to the death of the cross.*[108] For what reason but that *He became weak unto the weak, that He might gain the weak?* [109] Listen to His follower who in another place likewise says: *For whether we be transported in mind, it is to God; or whether we be sober, it is for you. For the charity of Christ presseth us, judging this, that one died for all.*[110] For how, indeed, would he be ready to be spent for their souls if he disdained to stoop to their ears? For this reason, then, *he became a little child in the midst of us, like a nurse cherishing her children.*[111] For is it a pleasure to murmur into the ear broken and mutilated words unless love invite us? And yet men wish to have babes for whom they may do this, and sweeter is it for a mother to chew morsels small and put them into her tiny son's mouth,[112] than to chew and consume large morsels herself. Therefore, let not the thought of the hen leave your mind, who with her drooping feathers covers her tender brood, and with tired cry calls her peeping chicks to her side; while those that turn away from her coaxing wings, in their pride, become the prey of hawks.[113] For if the intellect delights us by its penetrating to the very essence of things, let us also take delight in understanding how love, the more graciously it descends to the lowliest station, the more irresistibly finds its way to the inmost recesses of the heart, through the testimony of a good conscience that it seeks nothing of those to whom it descends, except their eternal salvation.

CHAPTER 11

The inadequacy of language to express thought must not discourage the catechist. Mistakes should be discreetly corrected. If he is misunderstood or meets opposition, let him remember the Lord's example.

16. If, however, we seek rather to read or hear such things as are already prepared for our use and better expressed, and for that reason find it irksome to suit our words to the occasion, in uncertainty as to the outcome; then, provided only that our mind does not wander from the substantial truth, it is easy for the hearer, if anything in our words offends him, to learn from the occasion itself how little it matters, provided the subject has been understood, whether the phraseology which was used expressly to make the subject clear, may not have been quite complete or appropriate. But if, though setting out with the best of purposes, we stray through human frailty from the paths of truth—although in catechizing beginners, where we have to keep to the most beaten track, such a thing cannot readily happen—still, lest perhaps this also should prove a stumbling-block to our hearer, it should appear to us to have occurred for no other reason than that God would test us, to see whether we can endure correction with calmness of mind, that we may not hasten to the defense of our error with a still greater error. But if no one tells us of our error, and if it entirely escapes the notice both of ourselves and our hearers, there is no cause for worry, so long as it does not happen again. But very often we ourselves, in calling to mind what we have said, discover some error and do not know how it was received when we said it; and so when love glows within us we grieve more if something, though false, was gladly entertained. For this reason, therefore, whenever an opportunity is found,[114] as we have reproved ourselves silently so we must in like manner take care gently and gradually to correct those who have fallen into some error, not through words that were God's but plainly our own. But if there are any who, blinded by insane jealousy, rejoice that we have erred—*whisperers, slanderers, men hateful to God* [115]—let them furnish us an occasion for the practice of forbearance and compassion, inasmuch as *the forbearance of God* also *leads* them *to penance.*[116] For what is more detestable and more likely to *lay up wrath against the day of wrath and revelation of the just judgment of God,*[117] than by an evil likeness and imitation of the devil to rejoice in another's woe?

Sometimes, too, although all is rightly and truly expressed, something misunderstood, or something which from its very

novelty is harsh because it is contrary to the belief and practice of a long-standing error, offends and disturbs the listener.
Now if this has become evident, and if he appears to be
curable, he should be cured without any delay, by an
abundance of authorities and reasons. If, however, the
scandal is unseen and secret, God's medicine is able to relieve
it. But if he draws back and objects to being cured, let us
then take comfort in that well-known example of Our Lord,
who, when men were offended at His word and shrank from
it as a hard saying, said even to those who had remained:
Will you also go away? [118] For it ought to be held firmly
fixed and immovable in our mind that, when the ages have
run their course, Jerusalem which is in captivity shall be set
free from the Babylon of this world, and that none out of her
shall perish; for he that shall perish was not of her.[119] For
the sure foundation of God standeth firm, having this seal:
the Lord knoweth who are His; and let every one depart
from iniquity who nameth the name of the Lord.[120]

If we bear these things in mind, and call upon the Lord
to come into our heart, we shall be less fearful of an uncertain
issue of our discourse because of the uncertain frame of mind
of our hearers; and even the very endurance of vexations for
the sake of a work of mercy will give us happiness, if therein
we are not seeking our own glory. For then only is a work
truly good, when the purpose of the doer is winged with love,
and as if returning to its own place, rests again in love. Moreover, the reading which delights us or the hearing of some
better language—although in our desire to set a greater value
upon it than upon the discourse which we ourselves have to
deliver we make our utterance labored or tiresome—will
render us all the keener and afford us more enjoyment after
our own efforts. Then, too, we shall pray with greater con-

fidence that God may speak to us as we desire, if we cheer
fully permit Him to speak through us as best we can. Thus it
comes to pass that *to them that love God, all things work
together unto good.*[121]

CHAPTER 12

*The boredom of repeating truths overcome by sympathy
for him who learns them.*

17. Again, if it be distasteful to us to be repeating over
and over things that are familiar and suitable for little
children, let us suit ourselves to them with a brother's, a
father's, and a mother's love, and when once we are linked
to them thus in heart these things will seem new even to us.
For so great is the power of sympathy, that when people are
affected by us as we speak and we by them as they learn, we
dwell each in the other and thus both they, as it were, speak
in us what they hear, while we, after a fashion, learn in them
what we teach. Is it not a common occurrence, that when
we are showing to those who have never seen them before
certain lovely expanses, whether of town or countryside,
which we through often seeing already have been in the
habit of passing by without any pleasure, our own delight is
renewed by their delight at the novelty of the scene? And
the more so, the closer the friendship between them and us;
for in proportion as we dwell in them through the bond of
love, so do things which were old become new to us also.
But if we have made some progress in the contemplative life,
we do not wish those whom we love to be delighted and
amazed when they survey the work of men's hands; but we
wish to lift them up to the contemplation of the skill or

design of the contriver,[122] and thence have them soar upward
to the admiration and praise of the all-creating God, in whom
is the most fruitful end of love. How much more, then,
ought we to rejoice when men now approach to study God
Himself, on whose account all things that should be learned
are to be learned; and how much more ought we to be
renewed in their newness, so that if our preaching as being
a matter of routine is somewhat dull, it may grow interesting
because of our hearers for whom it is all new. Then, to aid
us in the attainment of joy, there is moreover the thought
and reflection from what a death of error our brother is
passing over into the life of faith. And if we pass through
streets that are most familiar to us with all the cheerfulness
that springs from well-doing, when we happen to be pointing
out the way to one who had been in trouble through losing
his way, with how much more alacrity and with how much
greater joy, in the matter of salutary doctrine, ought we to
go over those things which, as far as we are concerned, need
not be repeated, when we are escorting through the paths of
peace a soul to be pitied, and one wearied with the wander-
ings of this world, at the bidding of Him who has given that
peace to us.[123]

CHAPTER 13

*The apathy of the listeners. The judicious catechist copes
with the difficulty.*

18. But in very truth it is a hard thing to continue speaking up to the point determined upon beforehand, when we
do not see our hearer moved. Since we who do not see into
his mind cannot tell whether he is held by religious awe and

dare not express his approval either by word or by some
gesture, or whether he is held back by natural shyness, or
whether he does not understand what is said, or considers it
of no value: so we must in our discourse make trial of everything that may succeed in rousing him, and as it were dis-
lodging him from his hiding-place. For we must drive out by
gentle encouragement his excessive timidity, which hinders
him from expressing his opinion. We must temper his shyness by introducing the idea of brotherly fellowship.[124] We
must by questioning him find out whether he understands;
and must give him confidence so that if he thinks there is
an objection to make he may freely lay it before us. We
must at the same time enquire of him whether he has ever
heard these things before, and so perhaps they, as being
things well-known and commonplace, fail to move him.[125]
We must then act in accordance with his answer, so as
either to speak more clearly and simply, or to refute a contrary
opinion, or not to set forth at greater length things that are
familiar to him, but instead to give a brief summary of them,
and to pick out some of those points that have been said
mystically in the Sacred Scriptures, and particularly in the
narration itself, the explanation and interpretation of which
may make our discourse more agreeable. But if he is exceedingly slow-witted, and out of accord with and averse to every
such inducement, we should bear with him in a compas-
sionate spirit, and after briefly running through the other
points, impress upon him in a way to inspire awe the truths
that are most necessary concerning the unity of the Catholic
Church, temptations, and the Christian manner of living in
view of the future judgment; and we should rather say much
on his behalf to God, than say much to him about God.[127]

19. It often happens, too, that one who at first was listening gladly becomes exhausted either from listening or standing, and now opens his mouth no longer to give assent but to yawn, and even involuntarily gives signs that he wants to depart. When we observe this, we should either refresh his mind by saying something seasoned with a becoming liveliness [128] and suited to the matter under discussion, or something calculated to arouse great wonder and amazement, or even grief and lamentation. And, preferably, let it be something concerning himself, so that pricked by the sting of personal concern he may arouse himself, yet something that may not wound his shyness by a suggestion of severity, but may win him rather by its friendliness. Or else we should come to his aid with the offer of a seat; [129] although doubtless it is better that he should listen seated from the first, where it can be done with propriety. And indeed in certain of the churches overseas,[130] with far more considerateness, not only do the bishops [131] sit when they address the people, but seats are supplied for the people also, lest anyone who is somewhat weak physically should become exhausted through standing, and so either should have his mind turned away from its most salutary design, or even be obliged to leave. It makes a great difference however whether someone, who has already become a church member by participation in the sacraments, withdraws from a large gathering, to recruit his strength; or one who has yet to be initiated in the rites of the catechumenate retires—a thing he is very often forced to do of necessity—lest he should be overcome by an internal weakness and even fall; for out of shame he does not say why he is going, and at the same time out of weakness he cannot keep standing. I say this from experience, for a man from the country did this once when I was catechizing him, and from this I learned that every precaution must be taken beforehand to prevent it. For who shall put up with our pride when we do not make

men, though they are our brothers, or even that they may
become our brothers (for we should be the more anxious in
this case), be seated in our presence, seeing that a woman
listened while seated to our Lord Himself,[132] before whom
angels stand and wait? [133] Of course, if the address is to be
short, or if the place is not suitable for a number to sit
together, let them listen standing; but this only when the
hearers are many in number and are not at that time to be
admitted to the catechumenate. For when there are one or
two or a few who have come with the express purpose of
being made Christians, we run a risk in keeping them standing while we address them. But if we have already begun in
this manner, at least when we notice our hearer becoming
weary, we should both offer him a seat, nay more, press him
by all means to be seated, and say something to refresh him,
and to banish uneasiness from his mind, should any breaking
in upon him have begun to distract him. For since the reasons
why he still remains silent and refuses to listen are uncertain,
let something be said to him, now that he is seated, against
stray thoughts about worldly affairs, either, as I have said, in
a light or in a grave vein. So that, if it is these thoughts that
had possessed his mind, they may withdraw as though accused
by name; but if it is not these, and he is merely weary with
listening, his flagging interest may be revived when we say
something unexpected and out of the common about these
thoughts in the way I have mentioned as though they were
actually the cause, when, as a matter of fact, we do not know.
But we should also be brief in this, especially as it is intro-
duced by way of digression, for fear that the remedy itself
should even increase the malady of boredom which we desire
to relieve; and we should both deliver more rapidly the remainder of our discourse and promise him a speedy conclusion—and then redeem our promise.

CHAPTER 14

You are interrupted in the midst of more congenial work? But this is God's work.—Compensation to God and to the catechist for grief caused by scandal.—The depressing consciousness of one's own sin or fault to be remedied by redoubled zeal for an unfortunate fellow man.

20. But if you are depressed over having to set aside some other occupation, on which you were already bent as being more important, and on that account are sad and catechize unattractively, you ought to reflect that, apart from knowing that in all our dealings with men we ought to act mercifully and in accordance with the duty of love unalloyed, apart from this, I say, it is uncertain what is more useful for us to do, and what is more seasonable, either to interrupt for a while or to stop altogether. For since we do not know what the merits of the men for whom we are exerting ourselves are in the sight of God, we can surmise only by the slenderest and most uncertain guess, if by any, rather than know surely what is good for them at the time. Therefore, we ought indeed to plan those things which we have to do as best we know how. If then we are able to carry them out in the way we intended, let us rejoice, not because it was our will, but because it was God's will that they should be so done. But if anything unavoidable happens to disturb our order, let us bend readily to it, lest we be broken; so that we may make our own that order which God has preferred to ours. For it is more proper that we should follow His will, than He ours; since even as regards the order which we desire to observe in performing our work, that order is of course to be approved in which the more important matters have precedence. Why then do we chafe that God, who is so much more excellent, should take precedence of us, who are but men, so that we desire to be rebels against His order through our very love for our own order? For no one plans what he is to do for the better unless he is readier to leave undone what is forbidden by divine power, than eager to do what is devised by human thought.[134] For *there are many thoughts in the heart of a man, but the will of the Lord shall stand forever.*[135]

21. But if our mind is troubled by some scandal and so is unable to produce a calm and agreeable discourse, so great should be our love towards those for whom Christ died, desiring to redeem them by the price of His own blood[136] from the death of the errors of this world, that the very fact of word being brought to us in our dejection that some one is at hand who desires to become a Christian should have the effect of alleviating and dispelling our grief, even as the joy over gains is wont to alleviate grief over losses. For we are not utterly cast down by the stumbling-block in any one's way, unless it be someone whom we see and believe to be perishing himself or causing a weak brother to perish. Let him, therefore, who comes to be admitted as a candidate wipe away our sorrow at another's defection, in the hope we cherish that he will make progress in the faith. For even if the fear suggests itself to us that the proselyte may become a child of hell[137]—as we see many such, from whom those very scandals that distress us arise—this should not tend to make us slacken our efforts, but rather arouse and quicken us to the point of warning him whom we are instructing to be on his guard against imitating those who are not Christians in very truth but only in name, and not to be stirred by their numbers either to desire to follow them, or on their account to be unwilling to follow Christ; and neither to be loath to be in the Church of God of which they are members nor wish to be such as they are. And, somehow or other, in such warnings that discourse has more fervor to which actual grief supplies the fuel. Thus, far from being dull, we say with more warmth and force what, were we free from anxiety, we should say somewhat flatly and sluggishly; and we rejoice that an opportunity is given us in which the emotions of our hearts may not pass away without bearing fruit.

22. But if for some error or sin of our own sadness seizes us, let us not only bear in mind that *an afflicted spirit is a sacrifice to God* [138] but also the words: *for as water quencheth a flaming fire, so almsgiving quencheth sin;* [139] and *for I desire,* He says, *mercy rather than sacrifice.* [140] As, therefore, if we were in danger from fire, we should, of course, run for water with which to extinguish it, and should be thankful if some one showed us water nearby, so if some flame of sin has arisen from the hay [141] of our passions and we are troubled about it, we should be glad when an opportunity for a work of great mercy is given us, as though a wellspring were pointed out to us from which to put out the blaze that had burst forth. Unless perhaps we are so foolish as to think we should run more readily with bread to fill the belly of a hungry man than with the word of God [142] to instruct the mind of him who feeds on it. Moreover, were it only profitable to do this, but not harmful to leave it undone, it would be an unfortunate measure to spurn the proffered remedy, when the salvation not now of our neighbor, but of ourselves, was involved. But since from the mouth of the Lord ring forth those words with so threatening a sound: *Thou wicked and slothful servant, thou oughtest to have committed my money to the bankers,* [143] what madness is it, then, because our sin pains us, to want to sin again by not giving the Lord's money to one who desires it and craves it? When by these and similar thoughts and reflections the darkness of disgust has been dispelled, our mind is prepared for catechizing, so that what bursts forth readily and cheerfully from the rich abundance of love is drunk in with enjoyment. For it is not so much I who say these things to you as it is love itself that says them to us all, that *love which is poured forth in our hearts by the Holy Ghost, who is given to us.*[144]

f) STYLE (CHAPTER 15):

CHAPTER 15

The style of the discourse should be adapted to the audience.

23. But now you also demand of me what I did not owe before I promised it, but is now perhaps due you, namely, that I should not count it irksome to unfold and set before you for your study some pattern of a discourse, just as though I myself were catechizing some one. But before I do this, I would have you bear in mind that the aim of one dictating [145] a catechetical instruction with a future reader in view is different from that of one catechizing with the listener actually present. And there is a difference, even in this latter case, between the aim of one admonishing in private, with no one else at hand to pass judgment, and of one teaching in public with an audience standing round that holds different opinions; and under this head again the aim differs when one only is being taught while others listen as if judging of and endorsing a subject familiar to them, and when all alike are waiting for what we are about to set before them; and yet again, in this division the aim differs when one and one's audience are seated together, as it were, in private, to begin a general conversation, and when a silent throng gazes with rapt attention upon one who is about to speak to them publicly. It likewise makes a great difference, even when we are speaking under these circumstances, whether there are few present or many; whether learned or unlearned, or a mixed audience made up of both classes; whether they are townsfolk or countryfolk, or both together; or a gathering in which all sorts and conditions of men are represented.[146] For it cannot fail to be the case that different persons should affect in different ways the one who intends to instruct orally and likewise the one who intends to give a formal discourse, and that the discourse which is delivered should bear a certain facial expression, as it were, disclosing the frame of mind of the speaker, and should affect the audience in various ways, just as the frame of mind varies, since they themselves mutually affect one another in various ways by their mere presence. But as we are now treating of instructing candidates, I can testify to you from my own experience that I am differently stirred according as he whom I see before me waiting for instruction is cultivated or a dullard, a fellow citizen or a stranger, a rich man or a poor man, a private citizen or a man honored by a public office, a man having some official authority, a person of this or that family, of this or that age or sex, coming to us from this or that school of philosophy,[147] or from this or that popular error; and in keeping with my own varying feelings my discourse itself opens, proceeds, and closes. And since the same medicine is not to be applied to all, although to all the same love is due, so also love itself is in travail with some, becomes weak with others;[148] is at pains to edify some, dreads to be a cause of offense to others; stoops to some, before others stands with head erect; is gentle to some, and stern to others; and enemy to none, a mother to all. And when someone, who has not in the same spirit of love experienced what I describe, sees that we are on the lips of the multitude in praise because some talent gives us charm, he accounts us for that reason happy. But may God, *before whose sight comes the sighing of the prisoners, behold our abjection and our labor, and forgive us all our sins.*[149] Wherefore, if anything in us has so pleased you that you want to hear from us some plan to be observed by you in preaching, you would learn this better by watching us and listening to us when actually engaged in the work itself than by reading what we dictate.

PART TWO

THE PRACTICE OF CATECHESIS
(CHAPTERS 16-27)

---

a) A MODEL CATECHETICAL ADDRESS (CHAPTERS 16-25):

CHAPTER 16

Our true rest is to be found not in the things of this world, but in God.

24. But still, let us suppose that someone has come to us who desires to be a Christian, and, while indeed one of the uneducated class, yet not a man from the country but a townsman such as you must come across in great numbers at Carthage; [150] and that, on being asked whether he desires to be a Christian for the sake of some advantage in the present life or on account of the rest which is hoped for after this life, he has replied that it is on account of the rest hereafter; we should perhaps instruct him by some such address as this:

"Let us give thanks to God,[151] brother; I congratulate you heartily and rejoice with you that amid the great and perilous storms of this world, you have bethought yourself of some true and assured safety. For even in this life men seek rest and repose from great labors, but because of their perverse desires they do not find it. For they wish to be at rest amid

52

things that are neither stable nor lasting; [152] and because in course of time these objects are withdrawn and pass away, they vex their victims with fear and anguish and allow them no rest. For if a man should seek to find his rest in riches, he is rendered proud rather than free from care. Do we not see how many have lost their wealth of a sudden, how many too have perished by reason of it, either through their eagerness to possess it, or because their wealth is carried off from them when overcome by yet more covetous persons? And even if these riches remained with a man all his life and never deserted their lover, he himself at his death would forsake them.[153] For what is the length of man's life, even if he lives to old age? [154] Or when men desire old age, what else do they desire but prolonged infirmity? So, too, the honors of this world; what are they but empty pride and vanity and the danger of downfall? For thus says Holy Scripture: *All flesh is as grass; and the glory of man as the flower of grass. The grass is withered, and the flower thereof is fallen away; but the word of the Lord endureth forever.*[155] Therefore he who desires true rest and true happiness must raise his hope from things that perish and pass away and place it in the Word of God; so that, cleaving to that which abides forever, he may also together with it abide forever.

25. " There are also men who neither seek to be rich nor go about striving to attain the vain pomp [156] of honors, but wish to find their pleasure and satisfaction in gluttony and debaucheries, in theatres and frivolous shows, which they have free of charge in great cities.[157] But thus they also both squander their small means in riotous living, and afterwards under pressure of want, break out into thefts and burglaries, and sometimes even into highway robberies, and are suddenly filled with fears both numerous and great, and they who a little before were singing in the tavern now dream of the sorrows of the prison. Moreover, in their eager pursuit of the games, they become like demons as they incite men by their cries to kill one another and to engage in furious contests, men who have done no injury to one another, but desire only to please a frantic mob; and if they observe that they are peaceably disposed, they straightway hate and persecute them, and raise a cry for them to be clubbed, on the ground that they are in collusion; and this wickedness they compel even the judge who is the avenger of wickedness to commit. But if they perceive that they wreak their most frightful enmity upon each other—whether they be what are called ' sintae,' [158] or actors and the stage-chorus,[159] or charioteers,[160] or common gladiators,[161] poor wretches whom they pit in a fighting contest against one another, not only men against men, but even men against wild beasts—and the fiercer the fury with which they perceive them to rage against one another, the more they love them and delight in them. They second them when in fury, and rouse it by seconding them,[162] the spectators themselves being madder against each other, as they second this combatant or that, than those whose madness they madly provoke, and whom they madly, too, desire to gaze upon. How, then, can the mind which feeds on dissension and strife preserve the health which comes from peace? [163] For as the food taken, so is the resulting state of health. Finally, though mad pleasures are no pleasures, yet of whatever kind they are, and however much the display of riches, the pride of honors, and the devouring gluttony of taverns, and the factions of the theatres,[164] and the uncleanness of fornication,[165] and the lasciviousness of the baths [166] give delight, yet one little fever carries all these things away,[167] and robs them of the whole vain happiness of their life while yet alive. There remains a void and wounded conscience which shall experience the judgment of God whose protection it disdained to have; and shall find in Him a severe Lord whom it scorned to seek and love as a gentle Father.

"But you, inasmuch as you are seeking that true rest which is promised to Christians after this life, shall taste its sweetness and comfort even here amid the bitterest afflictions of this life, if you love the commandments of Him who has promised it. For quickly will you realize that the fruits of goodness are sweeter than those of iniquity,[168] and that a man finds a more genuine and pleasurable joy in a good conscience amidst afflictions than he who has a bad conscience amid delights; for you have not come to be joined to the Church of God with the object of seeking from her some temporal advantage.

CHAPTER 17

Only one who approaches Christianity with a pure intention will achieve this rest. God's rest on the seventh day and in the seventh age.

26. "For there are some who wish to be Christians either in order to gain the favor of men to whom they look for temporal advantages, or because they are loath to offend those whom they fear. But these are reprobate; and if the Church bears them for a time, as the threshing floor suffers the chaff until the time of winnowing, yet unless they amend, and begin to be Christians for the sake of the everlasting rest hereafter, they will in the end be separated from her. And let them not flatter themselves because they are able to be on the threshing floor with God's grain, for they shall not be with it in the barn, but are doomed to the fire which they deserve.[169] There are also others who have, it is true, a better prospect, but are, nevertheless, in no less peril. These already fear God and do not mock the Christian name, or enter the Church of God with a feigned heart; but look for prosperity in this life, thinking to be more prosperous in earthly things than those who do not worship God. And so, when they see certain wicked and godless men flourishing and excelling in the prosperity of this world, while they themselves either do not have those things or lose them, they are troubled in mind as if they worshipped God in vain,[170] and easily fall away from the faith.

27. " But he who wishes to become a Christian for the sake of that everlasting blessedness and perpetual rest, which is promised to the saints as their future portion after this life, that he may not go into eternal fire with the devil, but may enter with Christ into His eternal kingdom, he is a Christian in very deed; wary in every temptation, that he be not corrupted by prosperity or broken in spirit by adversity, at once moderate and frugal amidst the abundance of worldly goods, and in tribulations courageous and patient. And he, moreover, as he advances will attain to such a mind that he loves God more than he fears hell; [171] so that even were God to say to him, ' Enjoy carnal delights forever, and sin as much as you are able, yet you shall neither die nor be cast into hell, but this only, you shall not be with me,' he would shudder at it, and would not sin at all, yet no longer to avoid falling into that which once he dreaded, but that he might not offend Him whom he so loves; in whom alone is that rest which *eye hath not seen, nor ear heard, nor hath it entered into the heart of man*—that rest *which God hath prepared for them that love Him*.[172]

28. " Now concerning this rest Scripture declares and

does not keep silent, that from the beginning of the world wherein God made heaven and earth and all the things that are in them, He worked six days and on the seventh day He rested.[173] For being the Almighty He could have made all things even in a single instant. But He had not labored to rest, when *He spoke and they were made; He commanded and they were created,*[174] but to signify that after six ages of this world,[175] in the seventh age as on the seventh day, He would be at rest in His saints; because they themselves will rest in Him after all the good works wherein they have served Him, which He Himself in them performs, who calls and commands them, and forgives their past sins and justifies him who before was ungodly.[176] For as, when by His gift they work well, He Himself is rightly said to work, so when they rest in Him, He Himself is rightly said to rest. For as regards Himself, He seeks no respite, because He feels no toil. But He made all things through His Word; and His Word is Christ Himself, in whom the angels and all the most pure heavenly spirits rest in holy silence.[177] Now man fell by sin and lost the rest which he had in His divinity; and recovers it in His humanity; and to that end at the fitting time, at which He Himself knew this should come to pass, He was made man and born of a woman. He could not be defiled by the flesh, of course, since He was rather to purify [178] the flesh. That He Himself would come, the saints of old learned by the revelation of the Spirit and foretold. And thus they were saved by believing that He would come, even as we are saved by believing that He has come, to the end that we might love God, who *so loved us that He sent His only Son* [179] to put on the low estate of our mortal nature and die at the hands of sinners for sinners. For even of old time and from the beginning of ages, the sublimity of this mystery ceases not to be prefigured and foreshown.

CHAPTER 18

The creation of all things. The creation of man and woman. Paradise.

29. " Inasmuch as God is almighty and good and just and merciful, He made all things good,[180] both great and small, both highest and lowest, both visible things, such as are the heavens and the earth and the sea, and in the heavens the sun and moon and the other heavenly bodies, and in the earth and sea, trees and plants and animals each after its kind, and all bodies celestial or terrestrial, and invisible things such as are the spirits by which bodies are animated and quickened. *He made man too in His own image,*[181] in order that, as He Himself by His omnipotence holds sway over the whole of creation, so man by his understanding, by which also he comes to know and worships his Creator, might hold sway over all the living things of the earth.[182] He also made woman to be his helpmate, not for carnal concupiscence [183]—since at that time before mortality, the penalty of sin, came upon them, they did not have perishable bodies—but that the man also might have glory of the woman when he went before her to God and might offer himself to her as an example for her to follow in holiness and godliness; even as he himself should be the glory of God,[184] in following His wisdom.

30. " And so He placed them in a certain place of perpetual bliss, which Scripture calls Paradise; and gave them a commandment, which if they did not transgress they should ever abide in that bliss of immortality; but if they transgressed it, they should pay the penalties of mortality. Now God foreknew that they would transgress it; but nevertheless, because He is the creator and maker of everything good, He made them more especially (since He made the beasts also) that He might fill the earth with the good things of the earth. And assuredly man, even as a sinner, is better than a beast.[185] And the commandment, which they were not to keep, He gave them especially that they might be without excuse when He should begin to take vengeance upon them. For whatever man does, he finds God worthy of praise in His deeds; [186] if he acts rightly, he finds Him worthy of praise for the justice of His rewards; if he sins, he finds Him worthy of praise for the justice of His punishments; if he confesses his sins and returns to an upright manner of life, he finds Him worthy of praise for the mercy of His forgiveness.[187] Why, then, should God not have made man, even though He foreknew that he would sin,[188] seeing that He was to crown him if he stood firm, make him conform to the divine order if he sinned,[189] and help him if he repented, being Himself at all times and in all places glorious in goodness, justice, and mercy? Especially since He foreknew this also, that from this mortal stock should spring saints who should not seek their own glory, but should give it to their Creator, and who being freed from all corruption, by worshipping Him, should merit an everlasting life, and a blessed life with the holy angels. For He who gave free will [190] to men in order that they might worship God, not of necessity as slaves, but of their own good will as free men, gave it also to the angels; and therefore not even did the angel who with other spirits, his henchmen, forsook his obedience to God through pride and became the devil, do any hurt to God, but only to himself.[191] For God knows how to make souls that forsake Him conform to the divine order, and by their justly deserved misery to furnish the lower parts of His creation with the most meet and

E 2

suitable laws of His wondrous dispensation. And so neither did the devil harm God [192] at all either by his own fall or by leading man astray unto death, nor did man himself diminish one whit the truth or power or blessedness of his Creator, because when his spouse was led astray by the devil into that which God had forbidden, he of his own will consented unto her. For by the most just laws of God were all condemned, to the glory of God through the justice of His vengeance, and to their own ignominy by the shame and disgrace of their punishment; namely, that man, who had turned away from his Creator should be vanquished and subjected to the devil; and the devil, when man should turn to his Creator, should be set before him as a foe to be vanquished; so that all who consented to the devil unto the end should go with him into eternal punishment; but that all who humbled themselves before God, and by His grace overcame the devil, should win eternal rewards.

CHAPTER 19

There were two cities from the beginning of human-kind. The deluge. Abraham, the chosen people. The saints under the ministry of the Patriarchs and Prophets were members of the Church.

31. " And we ought not to be disturbed that many consent to the devil, and few follow God; [193] for the grain, too, in comparison with the chaff, yields a much smaller amount. But as the husbandman knows what to do with the huge heap of chaff, so the multitude of sinners is nothing to God, who knows His purpose with regard to them, so that the administration of His kingdom may in no respect be disturbed or debased. Nor must we think that the devil has conquered because he has drawn away many with him only to be overcome, they with him, by a few. Thus there are two cities,[194] one of the wicked, the other of the just, which endure from the beginning of the human race even to the end of time, which are now intermingled in body, but separated in will, and which, moreover, are to be separated in body also on the day of judgment. For all men who love pride and temporal dominion together with empty vanity and display of presumption, and all spirits who set their affections on such things and seek their own glory by the subjection of man, are bound fast together in one fellowship; and even though they frequently fight one with another for these ends, still they are flung headlong by an equal weight [195] of desire into the same abyss, and are united to one another by the likeness of their ways and deserts. And again, all men and all spirits who humbly seek God's glory, not their own, and who follow Him in godliness, belong to one fellowship. And yet God is most merciful and long-suffering toward ungodly men, and offers them room for repentance and amendment.

32. " Likewise with regard to His destruction of all men by the flood, save one just man with his kindred whom He willed to preserve in the Ark, He knew indeed that they would not amend; yet during the hundred years that the Ark was building, the wrath of God, which was coming upon them, was at any rate preached to them,[196] and if they had turned to God, He would have spared them, even as afterwards He spared the city of Nineveh which repented, when He through His prophet had foretold its impending destruction.[197] Now this God does, granting an opportunity for repentance even to those who, He knows, will persist in their wickedness, in order to exercise and mold our patience with

Himself as our pattern; that we may thereby know how greatly we ought to suffer the wicked with forbearance, since we do not know what manner of men they may afterwards become, seeing that He, from whom nothing of the future is hidden, spares them and suffers them to live. Moreover, by the symbol of the flood,[198] wherein the just were saved by the wood (of the Ark),[199] the Church to be was foreannounced, which Christ, her King and God, by the mystery (of the wood) of His Cross, has buoyed up above the flood in which this world is submerged. Moreover, God was not ignorant of the fact that even from those who had been saved in the Ark there would be born wicked men who would once more cover the face of the earth with iniquities. But, nevertheless, He both gave a type of the future judgment, and foretold the deliverance of the just by the mystery of the wood. For even after this wickedness did not cease to sprout forth again through pride and lust and forbidden acts of ungodliness, when men forsaking their Creator, not only fell away to the creation that God made, so that they, instead of worshipping God, worshipped His creatures;[200] but even bowed their minds to the works of men's hands and to the devices of craftsmen, whereby the devil and his evil spirits[201] might triumph the more shamefully over them; for these rejoice that they are adored and worshipped[202] in such sculptured images, while they feed their own errors upon the errors of men.

33. "And even then, to be sure, there were not wanting just men[203] to seek God devoutly and vanquish the pride of the devil, citizens of that holy city,[204] who were made whole by the future humility of Christ, their King, revealed to them through the Spirit. Of these, Abraham,[205] a devout and faithful servant of God, was chosen that to him might be made the revelation concerning the Son of God,[206] so that by imitating his faith all the faithful of all nations in time to come might be called his children.[207]

" From him was born a people who should worship the one true God, *who made heaven and earth*,[208] while all the other nations served idols and evil spirits. In that people, without doubt, the future Church was much more clearly figured, for in it there was the carnal multitude which worshipped God for the sake of visible benefits. But in it there were also a few who thought on the rest to come and sought a heavenly home; to whom was revealed by prophecy the future humility of God, our King and Lord, Jesus Christ, that through faith in Him they might be cured of all haughtiness and swelling pride. Not only the words of these holy men who in point of time preceded the Lord's birth, but also their lives, their wives, children, and acts were a prophecy of this time, wherein through faith in the Passion of Christ the Church is being gathered together from the nations. Through the ministry of those holy Patriarchs and Prophets both these visible blessings, which they carnally craved of the Lord, were bestowed on the carnal people of Israel who afterwards were also called Jews, and likewise those frequent chastisements consisting of corporal punishments, whereby they might be frightened in due season, as was meet for their hardness of heart. And yet in all these things there were signified spiritual mysteries closely associated with Christ and the Church of which even those saints were members, although they lived before Christ our Lord was born according to the flesh. For He Himself, the only-begotten Son of God, the Word of the Father, equal to and coeternal [209] with the Father, by which Word all things were made, became man for our sakes,[210] in order that He might be to the whole Church what the head is to the body.[211] But just as while the

whole man is being born, even though he should put forth
a hand first in the act of birth, this hand is nevertheless joined
and fitted to his body beneath the head (just as also some
among the Patriarchs themselves were born with the hand
put forth first as a sign of this very thing), so all the just who
were on earth before the birth of Our Lord Jesus Christ,
though born before Him, nevertheless were united beneath
the head to that universal body of which He is the head.[212]

CHAPTER 20

*Israel's bondage in Egypt, Moses, deliverance through the
Red Sea, the Passover. The Decalogue. The city of Jerusalem, a type of the heavenly Jerusalem, founded. David.*

34. That people, then, was carried away into Egypt, and
served a most hard-hearted king, and schooled by the most
severe labors sought God as their deliverer,[213] and there was
sent to them one from their own people, Moses, a holy
servant of God, who in the power of God terrifying at that
time by great miracles the godless nation of the Egyptians, led
forth thence the people of God through the Red Sea, where
the water parted and made them a passage as they crossed over;
but the Egyptians, when they were pursuing them, were
engulfed in the waves returning to their bed and perished.
Thus, even as the earth was cleansed by the flood from the
iniquity of sinners who were then destroyed in that inunda-
tion, while the good escaped by means of the wood (of the
Ark), so God's people as they went forth from Egypt found
a way through the waters by which their enemies were com-
pletely destroyed. And here, too, the mystery of the wood
was not lacking. For Moses struck the sea with a rod that

this miracle might be wrought. Both are symbols of holy baptism,[214] whereby the faithful pass over into a new life [215] but their sins like enemies are totally blotted out. But even more openly was Christ's Passion figured in the case of that people when they were commanded to kill and eat a sheep, and to mark with its blood their doorposts, and to celebrate this rite every year, and to call it the Lord's Passover.[216] Most distinctly, indeed, does the prophecy say of our Lord Jesus Christ that *He was led as a sheep to be sacrificed*.[217] And with the sign of His Passion and Cross, you today are to be signed and sealed upon your forehead, as it were upon a doorpost; and so are all Christians signed and sealed.[218]

35. " Then that people was led through the desert for forty years. It also received the law [219] written by the finger of God, by which name the Holy Spirit is signified, as is most plainly declared in the Gospel.[220] For God is not limited by bodily form,[221] nor are we to think of members and fingers in His case, even as we see them in ourselves. But because it is through the Holy Spirit that the gifts of God [222] are apportioned among the saints, so that while they vary in power, yet they do not depart from the harmony of love; and because again it is in the fingers that a certain division [223] is especially apparent, yet without any separation from unity; either because of this or for some other reason the Holy Spirit has been called the finger of God; yet, when we hear this term, we must not think of the form of the human body. That people, then, received the law written by the finger of God on tablets which were, it is true, of stone,[224] to typify the hardness of their hearts because they were not to fulfill the law. For inasmuch as it was material gifts that they were craving from God, they were held more by carnal fear than by spiritual love; but naught save love fulfills the law.[225]

Therefore they were burdened with many visible ordinances, that thereby they might be weighed down as beneath the yoke of bondage, in the matter of observances in foods, and in sacrifices of animals, and in other things innumerable; all these, nevertheless, were tokens of spiritual things relating to the Lord Jesus Christ and to the Church. These were then understood by a few holy men so as to bear the fruit of salvation, and were observed in accordance with the fitness of the time, but by the multitude of carnal men they were observed only, not understood.

36. "And so through many and diverse tokens of things to come, which it would be too long a task to enumerate in full, and which we now see fulfilled in the Church, that people was brought all the way to the land of promise, there to reign in a temporal and carnal manner according to the measure of its longing; which earthly kingdom was, nevertheless, a figure of the spiritual kingdom. In it Jerusalem was built, the most illustrious city of God, which in her bondage was a type of that free city which is called the heavenly Jerusalem; [226] this word is Hebrew and is interpreted " vision of peace." [227] Its citizens are all the sanctified, who have been, who are, and who shall be; and all sanctified spirits, even all whosoever obey God with loyal devotion in the highest heavens, and do not imitate the impious pride of the devil and his angels.[228] The King of this city is the Lord Jesus Christ,[229] the Word of God, by whom the highest angels are ruled, the Word who took upon Him human nature that by Him those men likewise might be ruled, who shall all reign together with Him in eternal peace. As a prefiguration of this King in that earthly kingdom of the people of Israel, King David stood out most prominently, of whose seed according to the flesh [230] was to come our King in very truth, the Lord Jesus Christ, *who is over all things, God blessed forever.*[231] In that land of promise many things were done for a type of the Christ to come and of the Church; and these you will be able to learn gradually in the holy books.[232]

CHAPTER 21

The Babylonian captivity. Subjugation to the Romans. Continued prophecies of the deliverer to come—Christ.

37. " Yet after several generations He exhibited another type which was exceedingly pertinent to His design. For that city was made captive and a great part of it led away into Babylon. Now as Jerusalem signifies the city and fellowship of the saints, so Babylon signifies the city and fellowship of the wicked, since it is said to be interpreted ' confusion.' [233] We have already spoken a little before of these two cities running· on indistinguishably from the beginning of the human race to the end of the world, through the changing ages and destined to be separated at the last judgment. So the captive city of Jerusalem, and the people led forth into Babylon, are bidden to go into bondage by the Lord, through Jeremias, a prophet of that time.[234] And there arose kings of Babylon, under whom they were in bondage, who, having been stirred by certain wonders occasioned by their presence, came to know and worship and ordered to be worshipped the one true God, the author of all creation.[235] Moreover, they were bidden both to pray for those by whom they were held captive, and in the peace of these to hope for peace, for the begetting of children and the building of houses and the planting of gardens and vineyards. But deliverance from that captivity after seventy years was promised them.[236]

"Now, all this signified in a figure that the Church of Christ, in all His saints, who are citizens of the heavenly Jerusalem, was to be in bondage under the kings of this world. For the teaching of the Apostle also enjoins that *every soul should be subject to higher powers* [237] and that *to all men should be rendered all things; tribute to whom tribute is due; custom to whom custom,* [238] and so with other things which, saving the worship of our God, [239] we render to the rulers of the human order; since the Lord Himself, that He might afford us an example of this sound teaching, did not disdain to pay poll tax on the humanity with which He was invested. [240] Moreover, Christian servants and the good faithful are also bidden to serve their temporal masters with patience and fidelity, [241] whom they are to judge, if they find them doing wrong to the last; or with whom they are to reign as equals, if they likewise turn to the true God. Still, all are directed to be subject to human and earthly powers, until, at the end of the foreordained time, which the seventy years signify, the Church is delivered from the confusion of this world, as was Jerusalem from the captivity of Babylon. [242] And by occasion of this captivity even earthly kings, forsaking the idols for the sake of which they were wont to persecute the Christians, have come to know and worship the one true God and Christ the Lord, and it is on their behalf, even when they were persecuting the Church, that the apostle Paul bids prayer be made. For these are his words: *I desire therefore in the first place that supplications, prayers, intercessions, and thanksgivings be made for kings, for all men, and for all that are in high station; that we may lead a quiet and a peaceable life in all piety and charity.* [243] And so through these very kings peace was given to the Church, albeit temporal peace, temporal quietude for the spiritual building of houses and planting of gardens and vineyards.[244] For, behold, we too are now building up and planting you by this discourse. And this is being done throughout the whole world, with the permission of Christian kings, even as the same apostle says: *You are God's husbandry, God's building.*[245]

38. "And, indeed, after the seventy years which Jeremias had mystically prophesied [246] that he might prefigure the end of ages, and that the figure itself might nevertheless be renewed, the rebuilding of the temple of God was begun in Jerusalem. However, because all this was done in a figure, assured peace and liberty were not restored to the Jews.[247] Thus it was that they were afterwards overcome by the Romans and made tributary.[248] From the time indeed when they received the land of promise and began to have kings, lest they should think that the promise of Christ as their deliverer had been fulfilled in any of their kings, Christ was prophesied more openly in many prophecies, not only by David himself in the book of Psalms, but also by the other great and holy Prophets, until the day of the carrying away captive to Babylon; and in the captivity itself there were Prophets who prophesied that the Lord Jesus Christ should come as the deliverer of all. And after the temple had been restored at the expiration of the seventy years, the Jews suffered such great tribulations and afflictions at the hands of the kings of the Gentiles that they might understand that the deliverer had not yet come. For they did not understand that He should deliver them spiritually, but longed for Him for the sake of deliverance after the flesh.

CHAPTER 22

The six ages of the world. The sixth began with the birth of Christ. His Passion and Resurrection.

39. " So five ages of the world are ended.[249] Of these the first is from the beginning of the human race, that is from Adam, who was the first man made, to Noe, who built the Ark in the time of the flood. The second extends from that point to Abraham, who was chosen indeed as the father of all nations that should imitate his faith, but particularly of the future Jewish people, his descendants according to the flesh. This people alone of all the peoples of the whole world before the Gentiles received the Christian faith, worshipped the one true God; from which people also Christ the Saviour should come according to the flesh. For the epochs made up of these two ages constitute the principal subject of the books of the Old Testament; but those of the remaining three are also related in the Gospel, when the ancestry of the Lord Jesus Christ according to the flesh is recorded. For the third age is from Abraham down to King David; the fourth, from David down to that captivity in which God's people migrated to Babylon; the fifth, from that migration down to the coming of our Lord Jesus Christ. From His coming the sixth age is dated; [250] that at length the spiritual grace which at that time was known only to a few, the Patriarchs and Prophets, might be made manifest to all nations; that no one might worship God for material benefit, craving from Him not the visible rewards of their service and the happiness of this present life, but eternal life only, in which to enjoy God Himself; that in this sixth age the human mind may be renewed in the

likeness of God, even as on the sixth day man was made in
the likeness of God.[251] For then, too, the law is fulfilled when
all that it has commanded is done not from the lust of temporal things, but for the love of Him who has given the commandment. Nay, then, who would not aim to return the
love of the most just and merciful *God, who first so loved* [252]
most unjust and proud men, that for their sakes *He sent His
only Son,*[253] through whom He made all things, and who
being made man by no change of His substance, but by the
assumption of man's nature, should be able not only to live
with them, but even to be slain both for them and by them?

40. " And so He made manifest a new covenant [254] of the
everlasting inheritance, wherein man, renewed by the grace
of God, might lead a new life, that is the spiritual life; and
that He might show the first covenant to be antiquated,
wherein a carnal people living after the old man [255] (with the
exception of a few, Patriarchs and Prophets and some unknown saints, who had observed [256] it), and leading a carnal
life, eagerly desired of the Lord God carnal rewards and
received them as a symbol of spiritual blessings. And therefore I say,[257] did Christ the Lord, made man, despise all the
good things of earth, that He might show us that these things
are to be despised; and endured all earthly ills that He taught
must be endured; so that neither might happiness be sought
in the former nor unhappiness be feared in the latter. For,
inasmuch as He was born of a mother who, although she
conceived, was untouched by man and always remained
untouched, a virgin in conception, a virgin in childbearing,
a virgin in death,[258] was yet espoused to a workman, He put
an end to all the inflated pride of carnal nobility. Inasmuch
as He was born, moreover, in the city of Bethlehem, which
among all the cities of Judea was so insignificant, that even

today it is called a village, He did not want any one to glory in the exaltation of an earthly city. He, likewise, became poor,[259] to whom all things belong and by whom all things were created,[260] lest anyone believing in Him should dare to be unduly exalted because of earthly riches. He refused to be made a king by men,[261] because He was showing the way of lowliness [262] to those wretches whom their pride had separated from Him; and yet the whole creation bears witness to His everlasting kingdom. He hungered who feeds all,[263] He thirsted by whom all drink is created, He who is spiritually both the bread of them that hunger,[264] and the wellspring of them that thirst; [265] He was wearied with earthly journeying [266] who has made Himself the way to heaven for us; [267] He became as it were one dumb and deaf in the presence of His revilers, through whom the dumb spoke and the deaf heard,[268] He was bound who has freed men from the bonds of their infirmities; He was scourged who drove out from men's bodies the scourges of all pains; He was crucified who put an end to our torments; He died who raised the dead to life. But He also rose again, nevermore to die, that none might learn from Him so to despise death as though destined never to live hereafter.[269]

CHAPTER 23

The coming of the Holy Spirit. The first Christians. The conversion and apostolate of St. Paul.

41. " Then, having strengthened His disciples and having sojourned with them for forty days, He ascended into heaven in their sight; [270] and when fifty days from His Resurrection had been accomplished, He sent to them the Holy

Spirit [271] (for so He had promised), that through *the love poured forth in their hearts* [272] by Him, they might be able to fulfill the law not only without its being a burden but even with delight. Now this law was given to the Jews in ten commandments, which they call the Decalogue. [273] And these again are reduced to two, namely, that we should love God with our whole heart, and with our whole soul, and with our whole mind; and that we should love our neighbor as ourselves. [274] For that on these two commandments depend the whole law and the Prophets the Lord Himself has both said in the Gospel and made manifest by His own example. For in the case of the people of Israel likewise, from the day on which they first celebrated the Passover [275] in a figure by killing and eating a sheep, with the blood of which their doorposts were marked to preserve them unharmed—from that day, I say, the fiftieth day was completed when they received the law written by the finger of God, by which name we have already said that the Holy Spirit is typified; as after the Passion and Resurrection of our Lord, who is the true Passover, [276] on the fiftieth day the Holy Spirit Himself was sent to the disciples, [277] no longer, however, typifying the hardness of their hearts by tables of stone; but when they were gathered together in one place in Jerusalem itself, *suddenly there came a sound from heaven as of a rushing mighty wind,* [278] *and there appeared to them parted tongues as it were of fire, and they began to speak with tongues,* so that all who had come to them recognized each his own tongue (for to that city Jews used to come together from every land, wheresoever they had been scattered, and had learned the divers tongues of divers nations); then preaching Christ with all confidence, they wrought many signs in His name, so that, as Peter was passing by, his shadow touched a certain dead man, and he rose again. [279]

42. "But when the Jews saw that so many signs were wrought in the name of Him whom, partly through hatred and partly through error, they had crucified, some of them were incited to persecute the Apostles who preached Him; but others, marveling the more at the very fact that so many miracles were done in the name of Him whom they had mocked as crushed and vanquished by themselves, were converted by repentance in thousands and believed in Him. These were no longer in the state of craving from God temporal benefits and an earthly kingdom, and of looking for Christ, the promised King, after the flesh; but now they understood in an immortal sense and loved Him who in His mortal body endured so much for their sakes and at their hands, and forgave them their sins even to that of shedding His very blood, and by the example of His own Resurrection pointed out to them immortality as the object to be hoped for and craved from Him. And so mortifying now the earthly desires of the old man, and burning with the newness of the spiritual life, as the Lord had enjoined in the Gospel,[280] they sold all that they had,[281] and laid the price of their goods before the feet of the Apostles, in order that the latter might distribute them to everyone according to his need; and living together in the concord of Christian love, they did not call anything their own,[282] but all things were common to them, and they were one soul and heart towards God. Afterwards they too suffered persecution of their flesh at the hands of the Jews, their fellow countrymen according to the flesh, and were dispersed abroad, in order that by their dispersion Christ might be more widely preached,[283] and that they might likewise imitate the long-suffering of their Lord; for He who had suffered them in meekness, bade them, when they had been made meek, to suffer for Him.

43. " Of the very persecutors of the saints [284] had been Paul himself, the Apostle, and he raged most furiously against the Christians; [285] but afterwards he believed, and became an Apostle, and was sent to preach [286] the Gospel to the Gentiles, suffering more grievous things for the cause of Christ than he had committed against the cause of Christ.[287] Moreover, when establishing churches throughout all the nations wherever he sowed the seed of the Gospel, he earnestly exhorted them, that since they themselves, coming from the worship of idols, and uninstructed in the worship of the one true God, could not easily serve God by selling and distributing their goods, they should make offerings for the poor of the saints who were in the churches of Judea which had believed in Christ; [288] so the teaching of the Apostle constituted some as soldiers, but others as provincial taxpayers; [289] setting between them Christ as a cornerstone,[290] even as He had been foretold by the prophet, in whom both classes coming together as walls from different sides,[291] that is to say from the Jews and the Gentiles, might be joined in genuine love. But afterwards more grievous and more frequent persecutions arose from the unbelieving Gentiles against the Church of Christ, and day by day was fulfilled the word that the Lord had foretold: *Behold I send you as sheep in the midst of wolves.*[292]

CHAPTER 24

The Church of prophecy and history. How it has been watered with the blood of martyrs and pruned of heresies.

44. " But the vine which continued to spread abroad its fruitful branches throughout the world, as had been prophesied concerning it, and as had been foretold by the Lord Himself, burgeoned the more richly, as it was the more plenteously watered by the blood of the martyrs.[293] To these, as they died for the true faith in countless numbers throughout all lands, even the very kingdoms that persecuted them yielded, and when their stiff-necked pride had been broken, they were converted to the knowledge and worship of Christ. Yet it was needful that this vine should be pruned, as at sundry times had been foretold by the Lord,[294] and that from it should be lopped the unfruitful branches, by which, under the name of Christ, heresies and schisms were occasioned in various places, on the part of those who sought not His glory but their own, so that through their opposition the Church might be more and more tried, and both her teaching elucidated and her long-suffering tested.[295]

45. " All these things, then, we know have come to pass exactly as we read that they were foretold long before. And as the first Christians, because they did not yet see that they had come to pass, were stirred to belief through miracles; so we, because all these things have been fulfilled just as we read of them in the books that were written long before their fulfillment, when all things were spoken of as yet to be, and which are now seen in actual being, so we, I say, are edified unto faith, that, waiting and persevering in the Lord, we believe without hesitation that the things, likewise, which yet remain, shall come to pass, since we read in the same Scriptures of tribulations yet to come, and of the last day of judgment itself when all the citizens of both these cities shall receive again their bodies and rise and shall render an account of their life before the judgment seat of Christ, the Judge.[296] For He shall come in the splendor of power who before condescended to come in the lowliness of human nature; and He shall separate all the holy from the unholy, not only from those who have altogether refused to believe in Him, but also from those who have believed in Him in vain and without fruit. To the one group He shall give an eternal kingdom with Him, but to the other, eternal punishment with the devil. But as no joy in temporal things can be found in any measure like to the joy of eternal life which the saints are to receive, so no torment of temporal punishment can be compared to the everlasting torments of the wicked.

CHAPTER 25

Exhortations: to believe in the dogmas of the final resurrection and judgment; to lead a good life; to be unyielding to temptation and bad example; to associate with the good.

46. " And so, brother, strengthen yourself, in the name and help of Him in whom you trust, against the tongues of those who mock at our faith, out of whose mouths the devil speaks seductive words, bent, as he is, above all, on making a mockery of our faith in the resurrection. But from your own self receive the assurance that since you have been, so also you will be, since though before you were not, you see that you now are. For where was that mass of your body, and where that form and structure of your members a few years ago, before you were born, or even before you had been conceived in your mother's womb, where was this present mass and stature of your body? [297] Did it not come forth into the light from the hidden recesses of this creation, secretly fashioned by the Lord God, and rise by a regular growth through various stages [298] to its present size and shape? Is it, then, too difficult a thing for God, who even in a moment brings together from their hiding places the cloudbanks and overcasts the sky in the twinkling of an eye, to restore that substánce of your body as it was before, seeing that He was able to make it as before it was not? Believe, therefore, with a strong and unshaken conviction, that all things that seem to be withdrawn from the eyes of men, as it were, by decay, are safe and sound as regards the omnipotence of God, who shall restore them without any delay or difficulty, at His pleasure—those of them at least that His justice deems worthy of being restored—in order that men may render an account of their actions in those bodies in which they performed them; and that in them they may merit either change to heavenly incorruptibility as the reward of their goodness, or a corruptible state of body as the reward of their wickedness, a corruptible state of body not to be ended with death, but destined to furnish material for everlasting pains.[299]

47. " Flee, then, by steadfast faith and a good life, flee, brother, those torments in which the tormentors never weary and the tormented never die; to whom it is death without end not to be able to die in their torments.[300] And be on fire with love and longing for the everlasting life of the saints where neither shall work be toilsome nor rest slothful; where there shall be praise of God without surfeit and without stint; where there shall be no weariness of mind, no exhaustion of body; where, too, there shall be no want, either on your own part, to make you crave aid, or on your neighbor's, to make you hasten to his aid. God shall be the whole delight and contentment of the holy city living in Him and by Him, in wisdom and blessedness. For we shall be made (as we hope and expect, since it was promised by Him) equal to the angels of God,[301] and in equal measure with them we shall by vision at length have the fruition of that Trinity in which we now walk by faith.[302] For we believe that which we see not, that by the very merits of faith we may be counted worthy even to see what we believe,[303] and therein abide; that we may no longer shout the equality of the Father and of the Son and of the Holy Spirit, and the unity of the Trinity itself, and the manner in which these three are one God, in a profession of faith expressed in babble of words, but may absorb this by most pure and most fervent contemplation in that heavenly silence.[304]

48. " Keep these things fixed in your heart, and call upon God in whom you trust to guard you against the temptations of the devil. Beware too lest that enemy [305] steal upon you from some other quarter, who for the most spiteful solace of his own damnation seeks others to be damned with him.[306] For he makes bold to tempt Christians not only through those who hate the Christian name and who grieve to see the whole world in the possession of that name, and would still fain be in bondage to idols and diabolical superstitions; but also from time to time he endeavors to do so through those of whom we made mention a little while back, men cut off from the unity of the Church,[307] as when a vine is pruned, who are called heretics or schismatics. But yet sometimes he likewise attempts this, to tempt and lead men astray through the Jews. But this should be your greatest care, that no one be tempted and deceived by men who are in the Catholic Church herself, whom she endures as the chaff until the season of her winnowing. For *on this account is God long-suffering towards these,*[308] both that He may strengthen the faith and wisdom of His own elect by trying it through their frowardness, and because many of their number advance and taking pity on their own souls turn with great earnestness to the pleasing of God. For not all lay up to themselves through God's long-suffering wrath against the day of the wrath of

His just judgment; but that same long-suffering of the Almighty leads many to the most wholesome sorrow of repentance. But until that comes to pass, not the forbearance only, but also the mercy of those who are already keeping to the right way is schooled through them. Therefore you are like to see many drunkards, covetous, defrauders, gamblers, adulterers, fornicators, wearers of unholy charms, devotees of sorcerers, astrologers or diviners who are skilled in all kinds of unholy arts. Also you are like to notice that those crowds fill the churches on the feast days of the Christians which likewise fill the theatres on the ritual days of the pagans, and in seeing this you will be tempted to imitate them.[309] Yet why should I say ' you will see ' what you, of course, know even now? For you are not unaware that many who have the name of Christians do commit all these evil things that I have briefly mentioned. Neither are you unaware that men whom you know to be called Christians sometimes commit perhaps even graver offenses. But if you have come here with the idea that you may do such things, as it were with an easy conscience, you are much mistaken, nor will the name of Christ avail you when He begins to judge with utmost severity, who before deigned to come to your aid with uttermost mercy. For He foretold these things, and says in the Gospel: *Not every one that saith to me, Lord, Lord, shall enter into the Kingdom of Heaven, but he that doth the will of my Father. Many will say to me in that day, Lord, Lord, in Thy name we have eaten and drunk.*[310] For all, then, who persist in such works the end is damnation. When therefore you see many not only doing these things, but also approving them and persuading others to do them, put your trust in the law of God, and do not follow those that transgress it.[311] For not according to their way of thinking, but according to His truth will you be judged.

49. " Associate with the good, whom you see loving your King with you.[312] For you are like to find many such if such you yourself begin to be. For if at the public shows you desire the company and friendship of those who with you loved a charioteer, or a gladiator, or some actor, how much more should you delight in being associated with those who together with you love God, for whom he that loves Him shall never blush with shame, since not only can He not be conquered Himself, but He shall make those that love Him likewise unconquerable. Nor yet should you place your hope even in the good themselves who either go before you or accompany you on the way to God, since you ought not to place it even in yourself, however much progress you have made, but in Him who by justifying both them and you makes you such as you are. For of God you are sure, because He changes not; but of man no one can be prudently sure. But if we ought to love those who are not yet just, that they may become so, how much more ardently ought they be loved who are so already? But it is one thing to love man, another to put your trust in man; and so great is the difference that God commands the former but forbids the latter.[313] Now if you have suffered any insults or tribulations for the name of Christ and have neither fallen away from the faith nor strayed from the right path, you are destined to receive a greater reward; but those who in these things give way to the devil, lose even the lesser. But humble yourself before God that He may not suffer you to be tempted beyond your strength." [313a]

b) RECEPTION OF THE CANDIDATE INTO THE CATECHU-
MENATE (CHAPTER 26. 50):

CHAPTER 26

50. After the instruction you should ask him whether he
believes these things and desires to observe them.[314] And
when he answers that he does, you should of course sign him,
with due ceremony, and deal with him in accordance with
the custom of the Church.

As to the sacrament of salt which he receives [315] when it
has been well explained to him that the symbols of divine
things are, it is true, visible, but that invisible things are
therein honored, and that the species (of salt), when sanctified by the words of the blessing, is not to be regarded as it is
in every-day use, he should likewise be told what is meant by
the form of words which he has heard, and what the season-
ing element in it is of which this species of salt is the
symbol.[316] Next you should make use of this opportunity to
admonish him that if he hears anything even in the Scriptures that has a carnal ring, he should believe, even if he does
not understand, that something spiritual is therein signified
that has reference to holy living and the life to come. Now
this he learns in brief, so that whatsoever he hears from the
canonical books that he cannot refer to the love of eternity,
and truth, and holiness, and to the love of his neighbor, he
may believe to have been said or done with a figurative meaning, and endeavor so to understand as to refer it to that two-
fold love.[317] Of course, he is to understand " neighbor " not
in a carnal sense, but understand thereby everyone who may
be with him in that holy city, whether he be already there
or have not yet appeared. Nor is he to despair of the amend-

ment of any man whom he sees to be existing through God's forbearance, for no other reason, as the Apostle says, than that he may be led to penance.[318]

c) A SHORTER FORM OF INSTRUCTION (CHAPTERS 26. 51-27):

51. If this discourse, in which I have instructed a candidate as if present seems long to you, you may treat the subject more briefly; I do not think, however, that it should be longer. Though much depends upon what the actual case suggests, and upon what the audience present before you show that they not only endure, but even desire.[319] But when speed is required, see how easily the whole thing can be set forth. Suppose again that some one is present who wishes to be a Christian, and that when questioned, he makes the same answer as did the former candidate; for even if he does not so answer we may say that he ought to have so answered. Then the remainder should be treated of in the following manner:

52. "Verily, brother, great and true is the blessedness which is promised to the saints in the world to come. Yes, all visible things pass away, and all the pride of this life and the concupiscence of the flesh and the concupiscence of the eyes shall perish,[320] and they draw their lovers along with them to destruction. God in His mercy, desiring to deliver men from this destruction, that is, from everlasting punishment, if only they be not enemies to themselves and resist not the mercy of their Creator,[321] sent His only-begotten Son, that is, His Word, equal to Himself, by which Word He created all things.[322] And He, though abiding in His Godhead and neither departing from His Father nor being changed in anything, yet by taking upon Him human nature,[323] and appearing to men in mortal flesh, came unto men; that as death entered into the human race by one man [324] who was the first created, that is, Adam, because he consented to his wife, who had been led astray by the devil,[325] so that they transgressed the commandment of God; so through one man who is also God, the Son of God, Jesus Christ, after their past sins had been utterly blotted out, all who believe in Him might enter into eternal life.

CHAPTER 27

53. " For all things that you now see happening in the Church of God, and in the name of Christ throughout the whole world, were already foretold ages before.[326] And even as we read them, so also do we see them; and thereby are we edified unto faith. Once a flood took place over the whole earth, that sinners might be destroyed. And yet those who escaped in the Ark were a figure of the Church that was to be, which now floats upon the waves of the world, and is saved from sinking by the wood of the Cross of Christ.[327] It was foretold to one man,[328] Abraham, a faithful servant of God, that from him should spring a people who should worship the one God, amid the other nations that worshipped idols; and all things that it was foretold should happen to that people came to pass even as they were foretold. Christ also, the King of all saints and God, was prophesied in that people, that He should come of the seed of Abraham himself according to the flesh which He took upon Him, that all those also might be sons of Abraham who should imitate his faith. And so it came to pass: Christ was born of the Virgin Mary, who was of that race. It was foretold by the Prophets that He should suffer upon the Cross at the hands of that same people, the Jews, of whose race according to the flesh He came; and so it came to pass. It was foretold that He should rise again. He rose again. And according to the very predictions of the Prophets, He ascended into heaven and sent the Holy Spirit to His disciples. It was foretold not only by the Prophets but also by the Lord Jesus Christ Himself that His Church should be found throughout the whole world, being sown broadcast by the martyrdoms and sufferings [329] of the saints. And this was foretold at a time when as yet His name was unknown to the nations and where it was known, was mocked; and nevertheless, by His miracles (whether those He wrought in His own person, or those He wrought through His servants), while these are noised abroad and believed, we already see that what was predicted has been fulfilled, and that the very kings of the earth, who formerly persecuted the Christians, are now made subject unto the name of Christ. It was likewise foretold that schisms and heresies should issue out of His Church,[330] and under His name, wherever they might, should seek their own glory, not Christ's; and this too has been fulfilled.

54. " Shall not then those things that remain come to pass? It is evident that even as the former things that were foretold came to pass, so also shall the others, whatever tribulations of the good yet remain. So too the day of judgment which shall separate all the wicked from the good in the resurrection of the dead, and shall set apart for the fire which is their due not only those without the Church, but also the chaff [331] of the Church herself, which she must bear with utmost patience until the final winnowing. But those who laugh to scorn the resurrection, thinking that because this flesh rots it cannot rise again, are destined therein to rise again unto punishment; and God shall show them that He who was able to make these bodies before they were, can in a moment restore them as they were. But all the faithful who are to reign with Christ shall rise again in the same body in such wise as to merit being changed to angelic incorruption; [332] so that they may be made *equal to the angels of God*,[333] even as the Lord Himself promised, and may praise Him without any stint and without satiety, ever living in Him and of Him, with such joy and blessedness as are beyond both the words and thoughts of men.

55. "Do you, therefore, since you believe this, be on your guard against temptations (for the devil seeks some to perish with him),[334] so that not only may that enemy fail to seduce you through those who are without the Church, whether pagans or Jews or heretics; but also that you may not imitate those in the Catholic Church herself whom you see leading evil lives, either those who indulge without restraint in the pleasures of the belly and the palate, or the unchaste, or those given to vain or unlawful practices, or of shows or of diabolical charms and divinations, or those who live in the pomp and vanity of covetousness and pride, or who lead any life that the Decalogue condemns and punishes; but may rather associate with the good, whom you will easily find, if you also are such yourself; so that together with them you may worship and love God for His own sake, for He Himself shall be our whole reward, that we may have the fruition of His goodness and beauty in that blessed life. But He is to be loved not as anything that is seen by the eyes, but as wisdom is loved, and truth and holiness and justice and charity, and any other such virtues: not as these are found among men, but as they are in the very fount of incorruptible and unchangeable wisdom.[335] Whomsoever therefore you see loving these virtues, to them be joined, that through Christ who became man that He might be the Mediator between God and man,[336] you may be reconciled to God. But do not think that the perverse, even though they enter the walls of a church, shall enter into the kingdom of heaven; for in the time appointed for them they shall be separated, if they amend not.

" Imitate, then, the good, bear with the evil, love all; [337] for you do not know what he shall be tomorrow who today is evil. And do not love their wrongdoing; but love them to the end that they may attain to holiness; for not only is love of God enjoined upon us, but likewise love of our neighbor, and *on these two commandments depend the whole law and the prophets.*[338] And no one fulfills this law but he who receives the gift, the Holy Spirit, who is, in very truth, equal to the Father and the Son; for the Trinity itself is God, and in this God must all our hope be placed. In a man it must not be placed, whatsoever he be. For He by whom we are justified is quite distinct from those with whom we are justified. But not only through inordinate desires does the devil tempt us, but also through dread of indignities and sufferings and of death itself. Now, if a man suffers anything for the name of Christ and for the hope of eternal life, and endures it steadfastly, a greater reward shall be given him; but if he yields to the devil,[339] with him shall he be condemned. But works of mercy together with holy humility [340] obtain this from the Lord, that He suffers not His servants to be tempted above that which they are able to bear." [341]

NOTES

INTRODUCTION

1 That there were no divisions of the catechumenate and that the old theory of its having been distributed into four classes is based on a wrong interpretation of the ancient texts, has been shown conclusively by F. X. Funk (*Theol. Quartalschr.* 65 [1883] 41-77; 71 [1899] 434-43). L. Duchesne, *Origines du culte chrétien* (5th ed., Paris 1925) 310, follows Funk; cf. also M. Gatterer, *Katechetik* (2d ed., Innsbruck 1911) 22 f.

2 Cf. F. Probst, *Katechese und Predigt* (Breslau 1884) 44.

3 Cf. F. X. Eggersdorfer, *Der hl. Augustinus als Pädagoge und seine Bedeutung für die Geschichte der Bildung* (Freiburg 1907) 175; A. Eberhard, "Augustins Schrift De catechizandis rudibus in ihrer Bedeutung für die Entwicklung und den heutigen Stand der Katechetik," *N. kirchl. Zeitschr.* 17 (1906) 240. Note also Ambrose, *Exp. in Ps. 118, serm.* 18. 26: quia *rudes adhuc in fide*; earlier the deacon Pontius wrote concerning St. Cyprian as a candidate for baptism that he was *adhuc rudis fidei* (*Vita Caec. Cypriani 2*).

4 Cf. the treatise below, note 125.

5 These ceremonies would vary in various places; see Gatterer, *op. cit.* 24. In the present treatise Augustine says simply (26. 50): Quod cum responderit, sollemniter utique *signandus est et Ecclesiae more tractandus.*

6 Cf. M. Wundt, "Augustins Konfessionen," *Zeitschr. f. d. neutest. Wiss.* 21 (1923) 185. The traditional date, as assigned by the Benedictine editors, is ca. 400.

7 Cf. P. Rentschka, *Die Dekalogkatechese des hl. Augustinus: ein Beitrag zur Geschichte des Dekalogs* (Kempten 1905) 50.

8 Rentschka, *ibid.* 108.

9 Commenting on our treatise, N. H. Baynes (*Jour. of Rom. Stud.* 17 [1927] 135) remarks that "its psychological insight is positively startling."

10 Of this work the first two books and the first part of the third, in which Augustine proposed to write a guide to Scripture studies, were written in the year 397; the last half of the third book and

91

the fourth, outlining a system of homiletics, were added much later, about the year 426. On the time of composition, see H. Pope, *St. Augustine of Hippo* (London 1937) 371; A. Allgeier, "Der Einfluss des Manichäismus auf die exegetische Fragestellung bei Augustinus," *Aurelius Augustinus. Die Festschrift der Görres-Gesellschaft zum 1500. Todestage des Heiligen Augustinus* (Cologne 1930) 11.

[11] Cf. *De civ. Dei* 18. 23; also *De doctr. christ.* 2. 40. 61.

[12] Cf. Rentschka, *op. cit.* 62.

[13] Cf. P. Drews, "Der literarische Charakter der neuentdeckten Schrift des Irenäus 'Zum Erweise der apostolischen Verkündigung,'" *Zeitschr. f. d. neutest. Wiss.* 8 (1907) 226-33.

[14] A. Harnack in his book of selections from Augustine (*Augustin: Reflexionen und Maximen* [Tübingen 1922]), took five from our treatise: No. 36 (2. 3): Nam et mihi prope semper sermo meus displicet . . . ; No. 127 (12: 17): Iam vero si usitata et parvulis congruentia saepe repetere fastidimus . . . ; No. 437 (8. 12): maximeque commendans in scripturis canonicis . . . ; No. 440 (4. 8): Quapropter in veteri testamento est occultatio novi . . . ; No. 454 (26. 50): De sacramento salis quod accipit . . . .

[15] Cf. the treatise below, note 145.

[16] Cf. F. di Capua, "Il ritmo prosaico in S. Agostino," *Miscellanea Agostiniana* 2 (1931) 673; C. Mohrmann, *Die altchristliche Sondersprache in den Sermones des hl. Augustin* (Lat. christ. prim. 3, Nijmegen 1932) 17 f.

[17] His lectures: *Katechetische Vorlesungen über des hl. Augustinus Buch von der Unterweisung der Unwissenden in der Religion* (Salzburg 1830); his catechism: *Praktisches Handbuch der Katechetik für Katholiken oder Anweisung und Katechisation im Geiste des hl. Augustinus* (Salzburg 1832).

[18] *Die katechetische Methode vergangener Zeiten in zeitgemässer Ausgestaltung* (Vienna 1905).

[19] For a list of modern translations of the *De catechizandis rudibus*, cf. my earlier treatment of this work, p. xiv. To the versions given there I add: G. de Luca, *S. Agostino, La prima istruzione cristiana* (I libri della Fede 12, Florence 1923); S. Mitterer, "Büchlein vom ersten katechetischen Unterricht," *Des hl. Augustinus ausgewählte praktische Schriften, homiletischen und katechetischen Inhalts* (Bibl. d. Kirchenv. 49, Munich 1925) 229-309.

THE TREATISE

[1] "You have asked me": Augustine's *Confessiones* and the *De civitate Dei* were likewise written at the suggestion of friends. In fact, most of his works were occasional, arising in response to some specific need. For a very interesting account of the psychological starting-points of his principal works, see B. Legewie, *Augustinus, eine Psychographie* (Bonn 1925).

[2] "Brother" (*frater*): a term of affection in classical Latin which was applied by the early Christians to fellow believers who were united to one another by the bonds of affection, all Christians being brothers in the new life. Cf. 1 Cor. 16. 20 and 1 John 2. 9; Tertullian, *Apol.* 39; etc. It may be noted here that both St. Augustine and St. Optatus insisted on calling the Donatists *fratres*, though sinners and schismatics. The Donatists, however, refused to reciprocate.—Such compound names as *Deogratias, Adeodatus, Deusdedit, Quodvultdeus*, were common in Africa. They were apparently translations of Semitic names like Mattathia'ı (= "gift of Jehovah") or Nathanael (= "God gave"). A parallel in English is offered by such names as Praise-God Barebones, used by the Puritans in the seventeenth century.

[3] In classical Latin *ad aliquem scribere* meant "to write a book dedicated to someone." Cf. J. S. Reid's note (*M. Tulli Ciceronis De Senectute* [Cambridge 1920]) on *De sen.* 1, *aliquid ad te.* The deacon's request here was of course much more modest; he simply wanted Augustine to set down in writing and send him something on the method of catechizing. It was fortunate that Deogratias applied to Augustine, for quite apart from the latter's reputation as a theologian and writer, no ecclesiastic in Africa had had his experience with the various methods of catechizing. Augustine was familiar not only with the methods employed in Africa; he had likewise attended catechetical lectures both at Rome and at Milan.

[4] The verb *catechizare*, here meaning "to instruct," is derived from κατηχεῖν = "to teach," "to inform by word of mouth." The simple verb ἠχεῖν = "to sound" (trans. and intrans.), "to ring out," is found in Hesiod, Herodotus, and Euripides. The compound verb κατηχεῖν, which is composed of κατά intensive and ἠχεῖν, retained its root meaning "to sound down," but was applied to the act of informing and instructing by oral repetition; the idea being that children in school were instructed by making them "sing out" in

chorus the answers to the questions asked by the teacher. Κατηχεῖν in this meaning of "to instruct," "to inform by word of mouth," occurs first in Philo, *Leg. ad Gaium* 198. In the New Testament it is found in this meaning, for example, in Luke 1. 4; Acts 18. 25; Gal. 6. 6; among later writers, in Diogenes Laertius, Porphyry, etc. In the sense of giving instructions to catechumens it apparently occurs first in the oldest homily, the Ps.-Clementine, so-called *Second Epistle to the Corinthians* (17. 1), written probably before the year 150. The first Latin writer to use *catechizare* in the meaning of "to instruct orally" in the Christian faith, was Tertullian; e. g., *De cor. mil.* 9: quem Petrus *catechizat*. The word *catechismus* is first found in Augustine, *De fide et op.* 13.

The word *rudes*, here rendered "candidates for the catechumenate," has received special attention in the Introduction, p. 4.

⁵ Carthage was the primatial see of Northern Africa. The expression *apud Carthaginem* (for *Carthagine* = at Carthage) would lead us to infer that this treatise was composed at Hippo, Augustine's episcopal see, which belonged to the ecclesiastical province of Numidia. Cf. n. 150 below.

⁶ *Diaconus* (διάκονος), used here in its ecclesiastical meaning of one of the major ecclesiastical orders; cf. 1 Tim. 3. 12. In the early Church a man frequently remained a deacon for years, or for all his life, whereas today the diaconate is simply the last stage before priesthood.

⁷ The office of catechizing the *rudes* was sometimes performed by the bishop (cf. Ambrose, *Ep.* 33), but in most cases priests and deacons were the catechists (cf. John Chrysostom, *Hom.* 21 *ad pop. Antiochen.*). It must be noted, however, that, though laymen and those in inferior orders sometimes catechized, they were never permitted to do so in the church, but only in private dwellings or in catechetical schools, which frequently adjoined the church.

⁸ *Fides* in the Old Testament is used in its classical meaning of "trustworthiness," "conviction," "confidence," "reliance"; cf. Ps. 32. 4. Now, Christian writers had no exact equivalent to the active meaning of πίστις, for the substantive *credulitas*, derived from the adjective *credulus*, was used—at least in literary Latin—only in a bad sense. They, accordingly, hit upon the word *fides* as being the closest equivalent to the active meaning of πίστις, to designate the supernatural virtue of faith (cf. Matt. 9. 22: *fides* tua te salvam fecit). From this there was but a slight step to *fides* in its objective meaning of that which is believed: the Gospel, the whole Christian

religion. For the ancient meaning of *fides*, also as differentiated from πίστις, see the classical study by R. Heinze, "Fides," *Hermes* 64 (1929) 140-66; reprinted in Heinze's essays, collected by E. Burck: *Vom Geist des Römertums* (2d ed., Leipzig 1939) 25-58. Cf. also W. P. H. Hatch, *The Idea of Faith in Christian Literature from the Death of St. Paul to the Close of the Second Century* (London 1926).

[9] The classical divisions of an oration were the *exordium, narratio, probatio, refutatio,* and *peroratio*. Cicero defines the "narration" in *De inv.* 1. 27: *narratio est rerum gestarum aut ut gestarum expositio*. The rhetorical term *narratio* must have been applied long before Augustine's time to the historical exposition at the beginning of the catechetical instruction, otherwise Deogratias would hardly have used the term when writing or speaking to Augustine, and Augustine in turn would hardly have used it here without a word of explanation.—The *exhortatio*, mentioned a little farther on, was the practical application of the *narratio*.

[10] As early as 397 Augustine had shown in *Serm.* 9. 7 and 13 that he regarded the Decalogue as the norm of Christian morality. It is just possible that the deacon Deogratias was acquainted with this view of Augustine and had accepted it. On the other hand, it may be that by "precepts" Deogratias understood the "two-way" theory of morality which was still followed in catechetical works. However, though it is not clear whether by "precepts" Deogratias means the Decalogue or the moral law in general, there is no doubt that when Augustine uses the term, he is referring to the Decalogue.

[11] "Profession" (*professio*) is used here in its ecclesiastical meaning of "professing" or "confessing the faith"; leading a Christian life (*Christiana vita*) constitutes practice of the faith.

[12] For the earlier history of the title, cf. J. C. Plumpe, *Mater Ecclesia: An Inquiry into the Concept of the Church as Mother in Early Christianity* (Stud. in Christ. Ant. 5, Washington 1943). F. Hofmann, *Der Kirchenbegriff des hl. Augustinus* (Munich 1933) 264, points out that Augustine spoke of the "Mother Church" particularly to catechumens and the newly baptized.

[13] 1 Cor. 13. 12.

[14] The idea of the soul being imprisoned in the body is both Platonic and Christian. For the thought, see, for example, Cicero, *Tusc.* 1. 45, and Pliny, *Ep.* 1. 22. 7. Augustine has it also in his *Confessiones* 2. 2: *sed exhalabantur nebulae . . . et obnubilabant atque obfuscabant cor meum, ut non discerneretur serenitas dilectionis a caligine libidinis.*

[15] For the thought, cf. Dante, *Parad.* 19. 64-66:

lume non è se non vien dal sereno
che non si turba mai, anzi è tenebra,
od ombra della carne, o suo veleno.

[16] Night shall not encroach upon that eternal day. Cf. Apoc. 21. 5: et *nox ultra non erit.* The early Fathers of the Church, imitating the Apocalypse, were fond of describing heaven in terms of earth. Cf. Ps.-Cyprian, *De laude martyrii* (3. cent.) 21; Christi locus, ubi iacet gratia, ubi virentibus campis terra luxurians alumno se induit gramine et redolenti pascitur flore, ubi altum nemora tolluntur in verticem et ubi arborum densior coma vestit . . . . Omnia illic non frigoris nec ardoris nec ut autumno arva requiescant aut iterum tellus vere novo fecunda parturiat. Unius cuncta sunt temporis, unius poma feruntur aestatis: quippe cum nec mensibus suis tunc luna deserviat nec per horarum sol momenta decurrat *aut in noctem lux fugata concedat*; etc. Augustine, again, writes (*Enarr. in Ps.* 26. 7): *Dies vitae aeternae unus dies est sine occasu.*

[17] 1 Cor. 2. 9.

[18] Augustine now takes up the term *narratio* suggested by the deacon Deogratias (cf. above, n. 9), and sets out to develop it. He first recalls the division of the *narratio* as given by Quintilian 4. 2. 3: praeter haec alias (*narrationes*) perfectas, alias imperfectas vocant: quod quis ignorat?

[19] 2 Cor. 9. 7.

[20] From this expression we may infer that Augustine simply dictated this treatise without making any previous preparation, for in his sermons upon the psalms, which were frequently extempore, he often makes use of such phrases as *quantum Deus donaverit.* Cf. below, 15. 23 and n. 145.

[21] Augustine here answers the deacon's question (cf. n. 9) regarding the *exhortatio* by inserting it as part of the catechetical instruction.

[22] Cf. Gen. 1. 1.—Modern pedagogy could scarcely improve on the keen hints given in this passage as to how the subject matter of catechetics should be chosen, arranged, and presented so as to secure and hold the candidate's attention. How much psychology and logic are contained in the lines: ita ut eligantur quaedam mirabiliora, quae suavius audiuntur atque in ipsius articulis constituta sunt! For Augustine, applied psychology is the essence of catechetics, just as in oratory it is the essence of oratory (cf. Cicero, *De orat.* 1).

[23] Cf. Tertullian, *Adv. Marc.* 1. 10.

[24] The title of the Books of Kings in the Septuagint was Βασιλειῶν βιβλία, which was either transliterated or, as here, translated literally in the Old Latin version: *Regnorum libri.* Cf. also Cyprian who has *in Basilion tertio* (*Test.* 3. 62); note also *ibid.* 3. 80: *in Basilion* [variant: *Regnorum*] *tertio*; cf. again Ambrose, *Apol. David* 1. 2. It was Jerome who changed the title of these books in the Vulgate to *Libri Regum.*

[25] *Evangelium* is here used in its ecclesiastical meaning of "the Gospel." Cf. Matt. 4. 23: praedicans *evangelium.*

[26] For *articulus* used, as here, in the meaning of a "critical juncture," cf. Cicero, *Quinct.* 19; Pliny, *Hist. nat.* 2. 216; 18. 222; etc. For this meaning in Scripture, cf. Gen. 7. 13: in *articulo* diei illius; elsewhere in Augustine, e. g., *Conf.* 3. 9. 17 and *De civ. Dei* 16. 24.

[27] The ancient book was a roll of parchment. The Latins were fond of comparing the development of a thought to the unrolling ("evolving") of a manuscript. Note, for example, Cicero, *De orat.* 1. 16: sic modo *in oratione Crassi divitias atque ornamenta eius ingeni per quaedam involucra atque integumenta perspexi,* sed ea contemplari cum cuperem, vix prospiciendi potestas fuit. In the present passage, therefore, Augustine likens a catechetical discourse to the unfolding and spreading out of a manuscript.

[28] 1 Tim. 1. 5.

[29] Cf. Col. 1. 18: "And He is the head of the body, the Church."

[30] Elsewhere, in *C. duas ep. Pelag.* 3. 4. 10, Augustine says: *Huius generis fuerunt antiqui omnes iusti et ipse Moyses,* testamenti minister veteris, heres novi, *quia ex fide qua nos vivimus, una eademque vixerunt, incarnationem, passionem, resurrectionemque Christi credentes futuram, quam nos creuimus factam.* Note how in this treatise Augustine insists upon the intimate connection and interrelation of the Old and New Testaments: the Old Testament being but a preparation and a type and foretokening of the New. Note, likewise, how he makes our Savior the central object of both the Old and New Testaments.

[31] Rom. 9. 5. The Epistle to the Romans was Augustine's favorite epistle.

[32] The verb *apparere* ("to appear") is often used in classical Latin of divine apparitions and manifestations. Cf. Vergil, *Aen.* 2. 622: *Apparent* dirae facies, inimicaque Troiae/Numina magna deum. In Biblical Latin, however, *apparere* is the translation of the Greek verb ἐπιφαίνειν, which is frequently used in profane authors (e. g., Diodorus Siculus, Dionysius Hal., Plutarch) of the manifestation of

some god coming to the help of men, or again of the advent of a king to a city (cf. Herodianus 1. 7. 3). Hence, ἐπιφαίνειν, φανεροῦν, are used in the New Testament to describe the coming of Christ to save the world; for example, Titus 2. 11: *Apparuit* (ἐπεφάνη) *gratia Dei Salvatoris nostri omnibus hominibus*; again, 1 John 3. 5: *Et scitis quia ille apparuit* (ἐφανερώθη), *ut peccata nostra tolleret*. Augustine is, therefore, using this word in its Scriptural meaning (as in the present treatise again, 26. 52). On the subject see O. Casel, "Die Epiphanie im Lichte der Religionsgeschichte," *Bened. Monatschr.* 4 (1922) 13-20.

[33] 1 Tim. 2. 5.

[34] For this thought, compare Eph. 4. 11 f.: *Et ipse dedit* quidem . . . *prophetas . . . in aedificationem corporis Christi*; also Irenaeus. *Adv. haer.* 4. 55. 1: *Cum enim et ipsi* (*prophetae*) *membra essent Christi, unusquisque eorum secundum quod erat membrum, secundum hoc et prophetationem manifestabat*; cf. the same, *Dem. praed. apost.* 6; Augustine, *De. civ. Dei* 17. 16.

[35] Cf. John 1. 17.

[36] Cf. Rom. 10. 3.

[37] Ps. 19. 9.

[38] Col. 1. 18 (cf. above, n. 29).

[39] *Credendo in eum* = "by believing in Him": in classical Latin *credere* takes the dative of the person in the meaning of "to trust one," "to believe," "to take one's word." In ecclesiastical Latin *credere alicui* retains its classical meaning (as in Rom. 4. 3: *credidit Abraham Deo*, which is a literal translation of the Greek); *credere aliquem* = *credere aliquem esse*; *credere in aliquem* = "to believe in" and, as a result, "to love" (cf. John 14. 1: *creditis in Deum, et in me credite*, which is likewise in imitation of the Greek). For a discussion of these various uses, see Augustine, *Serm. de Symbolo* 1: *Non dicit, credo Deum, vel credo Deo, quamvis et haec saluti necessaria sint. Aliud enim est credere illi, aliud credere illum, aliud credere in illum. Credere illi, est credere vera esse quae loquitur; credere illum, credere quia ipse est Deus; credere in illum, diligere illum. Credere in aliquo* likewise occurs in the Scriptures in the meaning of *credere alicui* (cf. Acts 9. 42).

[40] Cf. Rom. 15. 4, 1 Cor. 10. 6 and 11. This composite of three different Pauline texts is illustrative of the puzzles that early Christian quotation from Scripture presents. *Ut nos doceremur* ("for our learning"): both the Vulgate and the Old Latin version read *ad nostram doctrinam; ut nos doceremur*, however, would seem to be the

reading of some early Latin version and not merely a casual para-
phrase of Augustine's, for it likewise occurs in C. Faust. 6. 9: Omnia
enim quae scripta sunt, *ut nos doceremur* scripta sunt. Et *figurae
nostrae fuerunt* ("and were lessons for us"): the Vulgate of 1 Cor.
10. 6 reads *haec autem in figura facta sunt nostri*; the Old Latin
version reads *haec autem in figuram nostri facta sunt*. The reading of
our text (*et figurae nostrae fuerunt*) would likewise seem to be taken
from some early version, for it occurs in C. Faust. 4. 2. Other words
and phrases in the quotation offer similar problems.

When Augustine wrote this treatise (*ca.* 405 A. D.) there were
two versions of the Scriptures in use: the Old Latin versions and
the Vulgate. It may be observed here that it is better to speak of
pre-Vulgate texts as the Old Latin version or versions (as there were
many; Augustine, De doctr. christ. 2. 11. 16: *Latinorum interpretum
infinita varietas*), to avoid endless confusion in the meaning of
"Itala." In 1896 appeared F. C. Burkitt's famous book, *The Old
Latin and the Itala*, in which he identified the much-discussed word
Itala of De doctrina christiana 2. 15. 22 (in ipsis autem interpretationibus, *Itala* ceteris praeferatur; nam est verborum tenacior cum
perspecuitate sententiae) with the Vulgate of Jerome and rejected
the theory that by *Itala* Augustine meant the Old Latin version (cf.
also Burkitt's article, "St. Augustine's Bible and the *Itala*," in *Jour.
of Theol. Stud.* 11 [1909] 258-68; 447-58). Burkitt's theory was
accepted by such great Biblical scholars as P. Corssen in a review of
The Old Latin and the Itala, in Gött. Gel. Anz. (1897) 416-22, and
by Dom de Bruyne in an article, "L'Itala de Saint Augustin," *Rev.
Bén.* 30 (1913) 294-314. Among recent writers who reject Burkitt's
theory may be mentioned R. P. Vaccari and A. d'Alès. Vaccari in
an article, "Alle origini della Volgata," *La Civiltà cattolica* (1915)
4; (1916) 1, suggests that in the obscure passage in De doctr. christ.
2. 15. 22: *in ipsis autem interpretationibus, Itala ceteris praeferatur*,
instead of *Itala*, we should read *Aquila*. This correction, however, as
d'Alès points out (*Novatien: étude sur la théologie romaine au milieu
du IIIe siècle* [Paris 1925] 38), does violence to the grammar of the
phrase, for it should be in the genitive: *Aquilae (interpretatio)*.
D'Alès (*op. cit.* 39) believes that *Itala* is a copyist's mistake for *illa*,
which fits in perfectly with the context. D'Alès is not the first to
suggest this new reading. It had been conjectured by the great
Bentley in 1734, but was rejected by the learned Benedictine, Dom
Sabatier. According to d'Alès, therefore, there was no "Italic Version," such as has been inferred from the existing text of De doctr.

christ. 2. 15. 22. From a study of the Scriptural quotations in Novatian, he concludes that there was an established Latin version of the Bible, which he calls *Vetus Romanum.* In this version the Old Testament is translated from the Septuagint; it is not, however, the same as that cited by the African writers. The Old Latin versions can be traced back as early as 250 A. D., though it is commonly admitted that a Latin version existed towards the middle of the second century. For recent summaries of these problems, cf. H. Vogels, "Bibelübersetzungen, II," *Lex. f. Theol. u. Kirche* 2 (1931) 303-7; J. E. Steinmueller, *A Companion to Scripture Studies* 1 (New York 1941) 168-75.

The Vulgate edition, which was prepared by St. Jerome at the invitation of Pope Damasus, appeared at intervals between 382 and 405. In short phrases, whether of the Old or the New Testament, where Augustine does not use a version but quotes from memory, he frequently gives the Old Latin text. This was only natural, since he was more familiar with the Old Latin version which he had used for at least six years in religious controversy and literary work before the appearance of the Vulgate revision. (A modern parallel case would be that of Newman who even after his conversion would naturally, unless he had the Douay version before him, quote from the King James version, which he had used for years and which he knew almost by heart). In the longer passages, where we may suppose he used a version, his Old Testament quotations were taken from an Old Latin version, while for quotations from the New Testament he used the Vulgate for the Gospels and for the Epistles a type of text represented in the Freising fragments (1). Cf. A. Souter, *Text and Canon of the New Testament* (New York 1913) 39; also de Bruyne, *Collectanea Biblica Latina* V (Rome 1921); for the Acts of the Apostles he employed the Old Latin version of St. Cyprian. The fact that in this treatise Augustine employed the Old Latin version for the Old Testament quotations, the Old Latin version of St. Cyprian for the Acts of the Apostles, and the Vulgate of Jerome for the Gospels, is in keeping with Burkitt's position (*op. cit.* 57), that "during St. Augustine's episcopate, from about 400 A. D. onwards, the Church read the Gospels from St. Jerome's version, though for the Acts it retained a very pure form of the Old African Latin."

[41] Bishop Robertson in his article on Augustine in *A Dictionary of Christian Biography* 1 (1877) 90, cites this passage together with *Ep.* 177. 15: *gratia Dei quae revelata est per passionem et resurrec-*

tionem Christi, to show that there existed in Augustine " a tendency to make the atonement not an efficient cause of redemption but a proof (to the elect) of God's love." The love of God for man is, of course, the ultimate cause of our redemption. This love God manifested to us through the Incarnation and death of Christ, for if He did not love us, He would not have sent His son. But this does not imply that the atonement on the part of Christ was not the efficient cause of our redemption.

[42] *Dilectio* is, strictly speaking, the equivalent of ἀγάπη, spiritual love, as opposed to *amor* (ἔρως), sensual love. Augustine, however, makes no such distinction in the use of these words; in fact he expressly controverts those who do. Cf. *De civ. Dei* 14. 7: hoc propterea commemorandum putavi, quia nonnulli arbitrantur *aliud esse dilectionem sive caritatem, aliud amorem.*

[43] Cf. Rom. 5. 8 and 10.

[44] Augustine here combines two different Scripture texts: 1 Tim. 1. 5 and Rom. 13. 10.

[45] Cf. 1 John 3. 16.

[46] Cf. 1 John 4 and 10.

[47] Rom. 8. 32.

[48] Concerning the verb *redamare* (lit., " to love back "), J. S. Reid, *M. T. Ciceronis De Amicitia* (Cambridge 1921), remarks that it was coined by Cicero (*De am.* 49). It does not occur again in classical Latin. For its post-classical use, see Ambrose, *In Luc.* 5. 75; Symmachus, *Ep.* 3. 2. For the thought, recall the hymn at lauds, Feast of the Sacred Heart: quis non amantem *redamet?* There are also the lines in Edmund Spenser's fine sonnet on the Resurrection:

> And that Thy love we weighing worthily,
> May likewise love Thee for the same again;
> And for Thy sake, that all like dear didst buy,
> With love may one another entertain.

[49] Augustine here contrasts the friendship (of the inferior person) which is based on *indigentia* and *miseria* with the friendship (of the superior person) which is based on *beneficentia* and *misericordia.* Cicero, while admitting that *amor* may be strengthened by the receiving of a kindly service, stoutly denies that mere utility and expediency can be the basis of a true friendship: cf. *De am.* 27-29; also 100. It is interesting to compare Cicero's definition of *misericordia* (*Tusc.* 4. 18): misericordia est aegritudo ex miseria alterius iniuria laborantis, and that by Augustine (*De. mor. Eccl. Cath.*

27. 53): quis ignoret ex eo appellatam esse *misericordiam, quod miserum cor faciat condolentis alio malo?*

⁵⁰ The verb *dignari* is often used in ecclesiastical writers of the condescension shown by a superior to an inferior; for example, by God to His creature.

⁵¹ Cf. Matt. 22. 40: "On these two commandments dependeth the whole law and the Prophets." Cf. also Augustine, *Serm.* 9. Augustine began insisting on the importance of the Decalogue, in this *sermo,* delivered in 397 (cf. above, n. 10). The complete presentation of the subject appears in *Contra Faustum.* Again and again in this treatise he emphasizes the fact that the Decalogue is the basis of all true morality, and that all the commandments may be summed up in the two great commandments of love of God and love of our neighbor.

⁵² *Memoriaeque mandata:* from the context it would appear that this phrase is to be translated "handed down as tradition." The classical expression for this is *memoriae prodere* (e. g., Cicero, *Brut.* 3). *Memoriae mandare,* on the other hand, means "to impress on the memory," (not "to learn by heart," for which the verb *ediscere* was used; example: Cicero, *Mil.* 78). In post-classical Latin many of these nice distinctions were blurred, if not entirely lost.

⁵³ The Latin—*in veteri testamento est occultatio novi, in novo testamento est manifestatio veteris*—is a splendid example of anaphora. This is one of Augustine's memorable sayings, more of which have passed into the common thought of Christendom than in the case of any other Father of the Church. Cf. Augustine, *Quaest. in Heptateuch.* 2. 73: *quamquam et in veteri novum lateat et in novo vetus pateat.* This assertion was directed against the Manichaeans who taught that the Old and the New Testament were in contradiction. Augustine at this time was just fresh from his work *Contra Faustum* (cf. above, n. 51), in which he had refuted the Manichaeans who were ridiculing the apparent contradiction between the Old and the New Testament, the "anthropomorphism" of Exodus, the Decalogue, the resurrection of the body, the semipagan attitude of many Christians, etc. A glance at this treatise will show that Augustine's head is still full of these controversies; in fact, there are whole passages in which he would seem to be addressing the Manichaeans rather than the *rudes.* Moreover, it must be borne in mind that Augustine himself was for nearly nine years a Manichaean auditor, during which time, as he tells us, he ridiculed the doctrines of the Church, especially concerning the Old Testament

Scriptures: cf. *De dono persev.* 20. 53, and *Conf.* 3. 18 (haec ego nesciens inridebam . . .); also read A. Allgeier, "Der Einfluss des Manichäismus auf die exegetische Fragestellung bei Augustin," *Aurelius Augustinus. Die Festschrift der Görres-Gesellschaft zum 1500. Todestage des hl. Augustinus* (Cologne 1933) 1-13.

[54] Cf. Rom. 8. 5.

[55] Cf. 1 Cor. 10. 3.

[56] In classical Latin *invidentia*—which word is used here—means the subjective feeling of envy; *invidia*, the objective feeling. Cf. Cicero, *Tusc.* 4. 16: *invidentia* utendum est enim docendi causa verbo minus usitato; quoniam *invidia* non *in eo qui invidet* solum dicitur, sed etiam *in eo cui invidetur*. This classical distinction is not observed by Augustine.

[57] *Mater autem invidentiae superbia est*: for the expression, cf. Cicero, *Acad. post.* 1. 39: omnium perturbationum arbitrabatur *matrem* esse immoderatam quamdam intemperantiam; also *De orat.* 2. 171, *Rep.* 3. 23, etc. With Cicero's personification of wisdom as mother (*De leg.* 1. 58) compare that by Origen (*Expos. in Prov.* 6; also *In Ierem. hom.* 14. 5). Augustine insists again and again on the wickedness of pride. Cf. his *In Ioan. Ev. tract.* 25. 16: *caput omnium morborum superbia est, quia caput omnium peccatorum superbia.* Regarding pride in the sin of Adam, see *De civ. Dei* 14. 13 and V. J. Bourke, *Augustine's Quest of Wisdom* (Milwaukee 1945) 266 f.

[58] *Humilitas* in the metaphorical sense of "lowliness" occurs in Cicero (*De inv.* 1. 56); in its Christian meaning it was, of course, unknown to the pagans. See Matt. 11. 29: Discite a me, quia mitis sum et *humilis* corde; also Phil. 2. 3 ff., 1 Peter 5. 5.

[59] Ut magnus *tumor* noster maiore contraria medicina sanaretur: note how Augustine plays on the literal and figurative meaning of *tumor*. The literal meaning of *tumor* is a swelling of the body (a "tumor"); the figurative meaning is a swelling of the mind ("pride"). The sovereign antidote for pride is humility. Cf. Augustine, *De doctr. christ.* 1. 13. 13: Sicut etiam ille qui medetur vulneri corporis, adhibuit quaedam contraria, sicut frigidum calido, vel humidum sicco . . . sic sapientia Dei hominem curans, seipsum exhibuit ad sanandum, ipsa medicus, ipsa medicina. *Quia ergo per superbiam homo lapsus est, humilitatem adhibuit ad sanandum.* Augustine sometimes refers to Christ Himself as *medicina, medicus*: cf., e. g., *Conf.* 9. 13. 35; *Serm.* 88. 13. For other references, see A. S. Pease, "Medical Allusions in the Works of St. Jerome," *Harv. Stud. in Class. Phil.* 25 (1914) 74 f.

[60] Cf. 1 Cor. 13. 13; also Augustine, *Ep.* 120. 8: Pia fides sine spe et sine caritate esse non vult; sic igitur homo fidelis debet credere quod nondum videt ut visionem et speret et amet.

[61] Cf. Ps. 110. 10: initium sapientiae *timor Domini.* While not neglecting the importance of a salutary fear, Augustine usually emphasizes love as being the special characteristic of the New Testament; cf. *De mor. Eccl. Cath.* 1. 56: Quamquam utrumque in utroque (testamento) sit, *praevalet* tamen in vetere timor, *amor in novo.*

[62] The practice of enquiring into the candidate's motives for wishing to become a Christian is much older than Augustine. Cf. *Traditio Apostolica* 40 (in T. Schermann, *Die allgemeine Kirchenordnung des zweiten Jahrhunderts* [Paderborn 1914] 54 f. [De novitiis ad fidem se convertentibus]): Qui in novam fidem introducendi sunt, priusquam populus advenit, atque *causa rei inquiratur, scilicet cur ad fidem sese converterint.* The *Trad. Apost.* dates from about 220 and is the work of Hippolytus. Its recovery, that is, as preserved in Coptic, Arabic, Ethiopic, and Latin versions, is owed to the scholarship of E. Schwartz (1910) and Dom R. H. Connolly (cf. his brilliant work: *The So-called Egyptian Church Order and Derived Documents* [Cambridge 1916]).

[63] The teacher must be tactful and sympathetic. Augustine remarks elsewhere (*Ep.* 22. 5): magis docendo quam iubendo, magis monendo quam minando.

[64] After the candidates has been questioned as to his motives and has given, for example, as his motive a divine admonition or divinely inspired fear, the catechist may take his cue from this answer and enlarge upon God's great care for us, and then proceed to the more solid road of the Scriptures. These two points are developed in the longer catechesis in Ch. 16. 24–17. 27 and Ch. 17. 28–25. 49. It is interesting to note that Augustine followed the same plan in recounting his own life in the *Confessions*; cf. 11. 2. 2: Quando autem sufficio lingua calami enuntiare omnia hortamenta tua et omnes terrores tuos et consolationes et gubernationes, quibus me perduxisti ... et olim inardesco meditari in lege tua.—As to the word "oracles" (*oracula*), St. Ambrose is fond of applying it to Scriptural utterances; cf., e. g., *De fuga saeculi* 20: in hymnis vel *oraculis.* The Benedictine editors in their note on this passage quote Philo's use of χρησμός in the same meaning: *De profugis* 2. 3. Most probably Ambrose's use of this word is in imitation of Philo (for Ambrose's indebtedness to Philo, cf. F. H. Dudden, *The Life and Times of St. Ambrose*

[London 1933] 113). Moreover, already in the first patristic document we possess, in St. Clement's *Epistle to the Corinthians*, another word for " oracle "—λόγιον—is so used; cf. 19. 1, 53. 1, and 62. 3 (see also J. A. Kleist's observation in his translation of Clement: ACW 1. 117 n. 179); and Clement, again, was known to Ambrose (see C. Schenkl's edition of Ambrose's works, CSEL 32. 1. xvii).

⁶⁵ The word *inhaerere* (here rendered " to apply oneself to ") does not occur at all in the Vulgate; but it is used frequently by the early Christian writers. It is a favorite word in the liturgy. Note, for example, in the Canon of the Roman Missal: et fac me tuis semper *inhaerere* mandatis; in the Secret *contra persecutores Ecclesiae*: divinis rebus *inhaerentes*.

⁶⁶ The candidate must not expect to be guided in his sleep by dreams, but by the Scriptures which he reads wide awake. Among the popular superstitions in Africa was a belief in dreams. Even among the African Christians, visions and dreams play an important part. Read, for example, Augustine's account regarding his own mother in the well-known passages: *Conf.* 3. 11. 19 and 6. 13. 23.

⁶⁷ Cf. Gen. 1. 31.

⁶⁸ The catechist, if he wishes to make the teaching of Bible history profitable, should not only narrate events, but should likewise search into their causes (*causas rationesque*): Augustine would, therefore, have the catechist insist on the philosophy of history. For the same conception of history, cf. Tacitus, *Hist.* 1. 4: ut non modo casus eventusque rerum, qui plerumque fortuiti sunt, sed *ratio etiam causaeque* noscantur. An insight into Augustine's philosophy of history is given by C. Dawson, " St. Augustine and his Age," *A Monument to Saint Augustine* (London 1930) 34-76.

⁶⁹ In speaking of the " grammarians " who were " good," Augustine seems to have had in mind the definitions of an orator given by Cato in his treatise *De oratore*: vir bonus dicendi peritus, and popularized by Quintilian, *Inst. orat.* 12. 1. 1: sit ergo nobis orator, quem constituimus, is qui a M. Catone definitur vir bonus dicendi peritus. The idea that an *orator* or a *grammaticus* must be a man of character, if he is to sway the minds of men, was always insisted upon by Greek and Roman rhetoricians in their disputes with the philosophers. Cf., e. g., Aristides, *Rhet.* 1. 2. 4; 2. 1. 5; Cicero, *De orat.* 2. 85. Cicero, however, does not deny that at times a man of bad character may be eloquent (cf. *De inv.* 1. 4). Christian writers, of course, followed the pagan rhetoricians in emphasizing the importance of character and good morals on the part of the *orator* or *grammaticus*.

Jerome is a good example (*Ep.* 69. 8): Sed futurus pastor ecclesiae talis eligitur, ad cuius conparationem recte grex ceteri nominentur. Definiunt rhetores oratorem: *vir bonus, dicendi peritus.* Ante vita, sic lingua inreprehensibilis quaeritur, ut merito suscipiatur. Perdit enim auctoritatem docendi, cuius sermo opere destruitur.

Concerning the *grammatici*: there were three grades in Roman education. The first, in which the elementary branches were taught, was presided over by the *primus magister* or *ludi magister*; the second, in which grammar and rhetoric were taught, had at its head the *grammaticus*; and the third, a sort of post-graduate course in rhetoric and philosophy, was in charge of the *rhetoricae magister.*

[70] The dogma of the resurrection of the body was particularly repugnant to the pagans and to various sects. See Acts 17. 33; also Origen, *Contra Cels.* 7. 33. Most probably Augustine has the Manichaeans in mind here. Noteworthy, too, is his statement in *Enarr. in Ps.* 88. 5: *In nulla re tam vehementer, tam pertinaciter, tam obnixe et contentiose contradicitur fidei Christianae sicut de carnis resurrectione.*

[71] Cf. Rom. 11. 22.

[72] Cf. Apoc. 21; also Gal. 4. 26 and Heb. 12. 22.

[73] Jews settled in great numbers in Africa after the destruction of Jerusalem. They were extremely hostile to Christianity and were responsible for many of the gross libels that were circulated about the Christians.

[74] Cf. Matt. 3. 12.

[75] Cf. Matt. 13. 30.

[76] Augustine is here referring to the Donatists. The Donatist schism began in 311 and flourished until the Conference at Carthage in 411. It was condemned at the Council of Arles, August 1, 314, and by the civil law in the very year in which this treatise was most probably written, 405; cf. *Cod. Theod.* 16. 6. 4. By the *turbae* here Augustine may have reference to the " troops " of the fanatical Circumcelliones whose vices and cruelties against the Catholic party were unspeakable. They had more than merited the harsh epithets which Augustine usually employs when speaking of them. Cf. *Ep.* 185. 15: *perditorum hominum dementissimi greges.* For other examples, see J. H. Baxter, " The Martyrs of Madaura, A. D. 180," *Jour. of Theol. Stud.* 26 (1924) 30. For the relations of St. Augustine with Donatism, cf. P. Monceaux, *Histoire littéraire de l'Afrique chrétienne,* 7: *Saint Augustin et le Donatisme* (Paris 1923).

[77] The word *conversatio* is here used in its ecclesiastical meaning

of "converse," "manner of life" (*Lebenswandel*). Cf. Phil. 3. 20: Nostra autem *conversatio* in caelis est.

⁷⁸ Augustine, like all the early Christian writers, was strongly opposed to the stage, because of its licentious character. Cf. Tatian, *Adv. Graec.* 22; Tertullian, *De spectac.* 10: saepe censores nascentia cum maxime theatra destruebant, moribus consulentes, quorum scilicet periculum ingens de lascivia providebant; *Apol.* 38; Clement of Alexandria, *Paed.* 3. 11. 76. 3–78. 1; Augustine, *De civ. Dei* 1. 32: ludi scaenici, spectacula turpitudinum et licentia vanitatum, non hominum vitiis sed deorum vestrorum iussis Romae instituti sunt. The theatre was extremely popular in Africa. How the youthful Augustine was attracted by it, is told by himself: *Conf.* 1. 10. 16; 3. 1. 1.

⁷⁹ The belief in astrologers (here termed *mathematici*) is frequently referred to by the Roman historians and satirists. It was of them that Tacitus (*Hist.* 1. 22) wrote: urgentibus *mathematicis* . . . genus hominum potentibus infidum, sperantibus fallax, quod in civitate nostra et vetabitur semper, et retinebitur. Cf. also Horace, *Carm.* 1. 11. 2; 2. 17. 17; Juvenal, *Sat.* 6. 553; Suetonius, *Tib.* 36. The Africans in particular were much given to superstitious practices and magical arts. Cf. Augustine, *Conf.* 4. 3. 4. In the breakup of the official cults during the first century after Christ there was a great influx of Orientalism to all the western provinces, and this included both religious mysticism and magic. These magicians fall into three main classes: (1) astrologers (*mathematici*), including fortune-tellers and compilers of horoscopes (*genethliaci*); (2) quacks (*iatrosophistae*), who professed to make cures by incantations and charms; (3) diviners and clairvoyants. Our principal sources for magicians and magic are the *Apology* of Apuleius and the *Confessions* and *De civitate Dei* of Augustine. Cf. A. Abt, *Die Apologie des Apuleius von Madaura und die antike Zauberei* (Giessen 1908); E. Doutté, *Magie et religion de l'Afrique du Nord* (Algiers 1910).

⁸⁰ These "diviners" were supposed to be able to recover lost property, detect robberies, read thoughts, and discover springs of water. One of the most famous diviners of the fourth century was Albicerius, to whom Augustine refers in *Contra Acad.* 1. 17.

⁸¹ Good Christians are the future "citizens of heaven." Cf. Eph. 2. 19: Ergo iam non estis hospites, et advenae, sed estis *cives sanctorum*, et domestici Dei. Cf. also Heb. 12. 22.

⁸² Cf. Ps. 77. 7. For Augustine's doctrine of justification, see J. Mausbach, *Die Ethik des hl. Augustinus* (2d ed., Freiburg i. Br. 1929) 2. 309 ff.

[88] The word used here, *iustificator* (= " justifier "), was coined by Augustine. For Augustine's contributions to the Latin vocabulary, see C. Mohrmann, *Die altchristliche Sondersprache in den Sermonen des hl. Augustinus* (Lat. Christ. Prim. 3, Nijmegen 1932), 159-164, 218-225 (223: *iustificator*).

[84] With this thought compare Tertullian, *De paenit.* 10: Cum te ad fratrum genua protendis, Christum contrectas, Christum exoras. Aeque illi cum super te lacrimas agunt, Christus patitur, Christus Patrem deprecatur.

[85] Cf. Rom. 5. 9.

[86] It is interesting to note that this is the only class of *rudes* that Augustine considers educated. With this class he contrasts those who come from the ordinary schools of rhetoric. For what these studies consisted of, see Cicero, *De orat.* 3. 127: nec solum has artes, quibus liberales doctrinae atque ingenuae continerentur—geometriam, musicam, litterarum cognitionem et poetarum; also Seneca, *Ep.* 88. 2: quare liberalia studia dicta sint vides; quia homine libero digna sunt.

[87] *Sacramenta* here refers to the initiatory ceremonies of the catechumenate, which consisted of exorcism, the signing with the Cross upon the forehead, the imposition of hands, and the administration of salt. Cf. L. Duchesne, *Origines du culte chrétien* (5th ed., Paris 1925) 313-15. There is perhaps no word in ecclesiastical Latin that has had so many significations and shades of meaning as *sacramentum*. In classical Latin it had the general meaning of " a solemn obligation, pledge, or oath." In the Scriptures, particularly in the Old Latin version, it is used to translate μυστήριον in the meaning of, 1) " a sacred ordinance, doctrine, or fact," 2) " a solemn obligation, pledge, or oath." It has, therefore, in its ecclesiastical use the general sense of " a religious mystery " (cf. below, Ch. 19 n. 206). For its various significations prior to Augustine, cf. J. B. Lightfoot, *The Apostolic Fathers, Part II: S. Ignatius, S. Polycarp* (2d ed., London 1889) 1. 51 f.; A. d'Alès, *La théologie de Saint Cyprien* (Paris 1922) 85-89; J. B. Poukens, " Sacramentum," *Bull. d'anc. Litt. et d'archéol. chrét.* 16 (1912) 10; E. de Backer, *Sacramentum, le mot et l'idée représentée par lui dans les oeuvres de Tertullien* (Louvain 1911); J. de Ghellinck–E. de Backer–J. Poukens–F. Labacqz, *Pour l'histoire du mot " Sacramentum ": 1. Les Anténicéens* (Spic. sacr. Lovan. 3, Louvain 1924); F. J. Dölger, " Sacramentum militae," *Ant. u. Chr.* 2 (1930) 268-80; J. Quasten, *Monumenta eucharistica et liturgica vetustissima* (Flor. Patr. 7, Bonn 1935-37) index, *s. v.*
The word has even a wider range of meaning in Augustine than

in Tertullian or Cyprian (cf. de Ghellinck, etc., *op. cit.* 16). He defines *sacramentum* in *Ep.* 138. 7: (signa) cum ad res divinas pertinent, *sacramenta* appellantur. In addition to the meaning in which it is used in the present passage, it may refer to the Lord's Prayer and the Creed (cf. *Serm.* 228); the chrism and imposition of hands (cf. *De bapt. c. Don.* 5. 28); Old Testament institutions generally (cf. *C. Faust.* 19. 16: *sacramenta Legis et Prophetarum*). Augustine defines *sacramentum* in its strict sense of a sacrament of the Church in his *In Ioan. Ev. tract.* 80. 3: Accedit verbum ad elementum, et fit *sacramentum*, etiam ipsum tamquam visibile verbum. He uses the word in this restricted sense in *De doctr. christ.* 3. 9. 13: Sicuti est *baptismi sacramentum, et celebratio corporis et sanguinis Domini; Serm.* 228. 3: De sacramento autem altaris sacri, quod hodie viderunt, nihil adhuc audierunt. Cf. J. Hymnen, *Die Sakramentlehre Augustins im Zusammenhang dargestellt und beurteilt* (Bonn 1905); C. Spallanzani, " La nozione di sacramento in S. Agostino," *Scuola Catt.* 9 (1927) 175-88, 258-66; H. M. Féret, " Sacramentum. Res. dans la langue théologique de saint Augustin," *Rev. des Sciences phil. et théol.* 29 (1940) 218-43.

[88] In keeping with a sound pedagogical principle, which was proverbial among the Romans: not to teach a man what he already knows; cf. Plautus, *Poen.* 880: *doctum doces*; also Jerome, *Ep.* 53. 7: *Stultissimum quippe est, docere quod noverit ille quem doceas.*

[89] From κανών = " a straight rod " or measuring line; hence, κανονικός = " regular," which in Latin transliteration becomes *canonicus*. In this meaning it occurs in Vitruvius 1. 1. 8. For a study of the word, cf. H. Oppel, Κανών. *Zur Bedeutungsgeschichte des Wortes und seiner lateinischen Entsprechungen*, regula-norma (Leipzig 1937).

Canonical, as applied to the Scriptures, means the books recognized as belonging to the list (canon) of Sacred Scripture, and hence constituting " the rule " of faith. Augustine in his works constantly refers to the importance of reading the *canonical* books only; cf., for example, *De doctr. christ.* 2. 8. 12: Erit igitur divinarum Scripturarum solertissimus indigator, qui primo totas legerit, notasque habuerit, et si nondum intellectu, iam tamen lectione, dumtaxat eas quae appellantur *canonicae*. Nam ceteras securius leget fide veritatis instructus, ne praeoccupent imbecillem animum, et periculosis mendaciis atque phantasmatis eludentes praeiudicent aliquid contra sanam intelligentiam. In *canonicis* autem Scripturis, ecclesiarum Catholicarum quamplurium auctoritatem sequatur; inter quas sane illae sint, quae apostolicas sedes habere et epistolas accipere meruerunt. Augustine insisted so much on this point because he knew how much harm had been done by the Manichaeans who read books not in the Canon of the Scriptures. The Synod of Hippo (canon 36), held in 393, prescribed that none but the canonical Scriptures should be read in church.

[90] Speaking of Holy Scriptures, Augustine writes in *De doctr. christ.* 4. 6. 9: *Quanto videtur humilior, tanto altius non ventositate, sed soliditate transcendit.* Augustine's first impressions of Holy Scripture, gained from the Old Latin version, were unfavorable, its crude diction and homely construction grating on his ear. It must be borne in mind that the Old Latin version was made for the lower, uneducated classes, from which a great number of Christians came. It had therefore to be written in the *sermo plebeius.* Augustine's reaction from reading the Scriptures is thus described in *Conf.* 3. 5. 9: Institui animum intendere in scripturas sanctas, et videre quales essent . . . (*scriptura*) *visa est mihi indigna, quam Tullianae dignitati compararem.* This simplicity and homeliness in the language of Scripture was one of the principal factors in prejudicing educated pagans against Christianity. Cf. Lactantius, *Inst. div.* 5. 1. 15: Haec imprimis causa est, cur apud sapientes et doctos et principes huius saeculi scriptura sancta fide careat, quod prophetae communi ac simplici sermone, ut ad populum, sunt locuti . . . With Augustine's conversion there came to him a new conception of the functions of language and style, that of bringing to all men the truths of the Gospel. If this one supreme object could be attained, he was more than willing to sacrifice elegance, and even correctness, of diction. Cf. *Enarr. in Ps.* 128. 20: Melius est reprehendant nos grammatici, quam non intelligant populi; *De doctr. christ.* 3. 3. 7: Plerumque loquendi consuetudo vulgaris utilior est significandis rebus quam antiquitas literata; *Enarr. in Ps.* 123. 8: saepe enim verba non Latina pono, ut vos intelligatis. In the language of Scripture Augustine found a vehicle of expression familiar to Christians of the lowest station upon whom the beauty of classical Latin would have been lost. Augustine moreover, imitated the language and style of Scripture for the reason that not only the subject matter but the very form of Scripture, its idioms and syntax, however much at variance with classical usage, were sacred in his eyes, inasmuch as they were the inspired word of God. For this reason, that he considered the language of the Old Latin version to be inspired, St. Augustine held out for a long time before accepting Jerome's revision (cf. *Ep.* 121.

28; *De doctr. christ.* 2. 15. 22). Moreover, Augustine was quick to see that classical Latin with all its majesty and hard brilliancy was stiff and unspiritual, the language of soldiers and jurists, but not the language of the soul; while the Latin of the Scriptures, saturated with Hebraic emotion and imagery, was the proper vehicle to convey "the outpourings of mystical devotion, to catch the elusive quality of shadowy moods, to enter into the subtleties of psychological analysis." Augustine, therefore, thanks to Holy Scripture, was able to give the Latin language a soul. Harnack, in *Augustin: Reflexionen und Maximen* (Tübingen 1922) 5, writes: "Erst er hat aus der lateinischen Sprache ein seelisches Instrument gemacht und ihr und deren Töchtersprachen, ja auch den germanischen, die christliche Seele und die Rede des Herzens gegeben."

[91] The word is used here in its ecclesiastical meaning of "catholic," "orthodox." Cf. Prudentius, *Peristeph.* 11. 24.

[92] *Communio* is here used in its ecclesiastical meaning of "being in communion with the Church." Just two years prior to the writing of this treatise, in 403, Augustine had composed his famous treatise *De unitate Ecclesiae* against the Donatists.

[93] For an illustration of Augustine's tolerance and charity towards heretics and schismatics who were in good faith, see *Ep.* 43. 1 (written in 398): Sed qui sententiam suam, quamvis falsam atque perversam, nulla pertinaci animositate defendunt, praesertim quam non audacia praesumptionis suae pepererunt, sed a seductis atque in errorem lapsis parentibus acceperunt, quaerunt autem cauta sollicitudine veritatem, corrigi parati, cum invenerint; nequaquam sunt inter haereticos deputandi.—Later on, however, he favored coercion as being the only possible way of dealing with the Donatists. Cf. *Ep.* 93 (written in 408).

[94] That is, to charity (cf. 1 Cor. 12. 31).

[95] According to Augustine, those who present themselves for instruction fall into three classes: the well-educated (cf. Ch. 8 n. 86); the half-educated, who come from second-rate schools of rhetoric (*quidam de scholis usitatissimis*); and the illiterate, *idiotae*. It is in this passage especially that Augustine shows the result of his own wide culture and knowledge of the world as well as his truly Christian modesty and tact. After his experience as student at Carthage, professor of rhetoric at Rome and Milan, and bishop at Hippo, he was well qualified to speak of these three classes of candidates. He once more makes it clear that he regards only the *liberalibus doctrinis exculti* (cf. Ch. 8 n. 86) as really educated: *illos doctissimos*, etc.

With the half-educated, the products of the rhetorical schools, he is most severe. This is only another indication of how vehemently he was opposed to the vicious system of rhetorical education, so popular in his time, which substituted words for ideas and fustian for literature, and how anxious he was to revive the educational ideals set forth in Cicero's *De oratore*. Augustine, following Cicero, considers a liberal education to be the only education worthy of the name. His services, therefore, to Christian education cannot be easily estimated; it was he who carried over into the Church the best classical tradition.

[96] The pagans, and sometimes wordly Christians, preferred purity of diction to purity of life. Cf. Augustine, *Conf.* 1. 18. 28: Quid autem mirum . . . quando mihi imitandi proponebantur homines, qui aliqua facta sua non mala, si cum barbarismo aut soloecismo enuntiarent, reprehensi confundebantur; si autem libidines suas integris et rite consequentibus verbis copiose ordinateque narrarent, laudati gloriabantur? In *C. adv. Leg. et Proph.* 1. 52 Augustine describes God as being: magis morum quam verborum pulchritudinem quaerens atque munditiam.

Statements such as these, quoted out of their context, in which the Christian Fathers seem to depreciate all secular knowledge, are frequently adduced to prove that Christianity was hostile to all learning and science. Prof. W. R. Halliday in *The Pagan Background of Early Christianity* (London 1925) 171 f., sums up the case very fairly when he observes: " It is not generally true of the Fathers that they were enemies of learning or science; they were themselves, for the most part, among the learned men of their day. If a Puritan wing of Christianity in extreme reaction against intellectualism preached the complete worthlessness of secular scientific knowledge, an extreme party among the Pagans did much the same. In either case the attitude was prompted by a genuine sense of the spiritual needs of contemporary life and their paramount importance, which lent a real force to their preaching. The perception of this no doubt affected, and legitimately affected, the occasional utterances of the more philosophic preachers, both Pagan and Christian, but it finds expression in impatient overstatements of the moment rather than forms part of the consistent structure of their thought "; see also A. S. Pease, " The Attitude of Jerome towards Pagan Literature," *Trans. Am. Phil. Ass.* 50 (1919), 150-67.

[97] For the thought, cf. Augustine, *De doctr. christ.* 4. 6. 9, when speaking of the eloquence of Sacred Scripture: alios autem, quanto

videtur humilior, tanto altius non ventositate, sed soliditate transcendit. The eloquence of the sacred writers is perfect, inasmuch
as their style and diction is perfectly adapted to their subjects. Any
educated reader of Augustine's time must have recognized that he
was here alluding to the pomposity of the Sophistic rhetoric without
mentioning it by name.—*Eloquium* (= " diction "), a favorite word
in Scripture, is frequently used by the Fathers to designate Holy
Scripture itself.

[98] Augustine never tires of emphasizing the pedagogical value of
allegorism. In this he was influenced by St. Ambrose, who first
established it in the Western Church; Augustine, however, was
much more moderate than Ambrose in its use. Cf. P. de Labriolle,
" Saint Ambroise et l'exégèse allégorique," *Annales de philos. chrét.*
155 (1908) 591-603; D. Haugg, " Augustinus und die Bibel," *Theol.
u. Glaube* 29 (1937) 373-90; P. Asslaber, *Die persönlichen Bezie-
hungen der drei grossen Kirchenlehrer Ambrosius, Hieronymus und
Augustinus* (Vienna 1908) 35.

[99] Augustine himself tells us that when he first went to hear St.
Ambrose preach he was not so much interested in *what* he said as
in *how* he said it: *et verbis eius suspendebar intentus, rerum autem
incuriosus et contemptor adstabam* (*Conf.* 5. 13. 23).

[100] Cf. *Enarr. in Ps.* 30, *serm.* 3. 10: Clamor ad Deum non est
voce, sed corde.

[101] *Antistes* is sometimes used absolutely by Augustine for " bishop "
(e. g., *Conf.* 9. 7. 16, with reference to Ambrose), and occasionally
in its metaphorical sense (e. g., *Conf.* 6. 2. 2: praedicatore atque
antistite pietatis). In the present passage, however, I believe that
antistites et ministros ecclesiae is pleonastic for " ministers," the
officiating clerics, of the Church, in general. For a similar use of
this phrase, cf. Augustine, *De mor. Eccl. Cath.* 1. 1. Augustine,
then, has reference here to the clergy in general, whether bishops,
priests, deacons, or clerics in minor orders. North Africa in Augustine's day was a strange mixture of languages and nationalities.
Valerius, Augustine's predecessor in the see of Hippo, was a Greek,
and preached in Latin only with great difficulty. Many of the
priests knew only their native Punic and spoke Latin very poorly
and with a strong Punic accent. Augustine himself tells us (*De
ordine* 2. 17. 45) that he spoke Latin with a provincial accent. Punic,
of course, he knew thoroughly, it being his native tongue. Cf. O.
Rottmanner, " Zur Sprachenkenntnis des hl. Augustinus," *Theol.
Quartalschr.* 12 (1895) 269-76 (reprinted in *Geistesfrüchte aus der
Klosterzelle* [Munich 1908] 61-66).

[102] *Christiano nomine* = "in the Christian faith": *nomen* in Latin connotes all that goes with the name; for instance, *nomen Romanum* = "the Roman nation, dominion, power, prestige." Cf. Sallust, *Cat.* 52. 24: gens infestissima *nomini Romano. Christiano nomine* here, therefore, designates the Christian religion. Cf. Tertullian, *Apol.* 5: *nomen Christianum* in saeculum introivit.

[103] The doubtful outcome of the speech is one of the things that disturbs even the greatest orator, according to Cicero (*De orat.* 1. 26).

[104] Augustine was always on the lookout for signs and gestures that would show that his hearers were following him (cf. *De doctr. christ.* 4. 10. 25). As a rule the African nature was very quick to show its approbation; in fact, Augustine had often to reprove his congregation for breaking out into applause and cheers when something in his sermon pleased them. In *Serm.* 339. 1, Augustine gives a very ingenious account of his attitude towards applause on the part of the congregation: Laudari autem a male viventibus nolo, abhorreo, detestor: dolori mihi est, non voluptati. Laudari autem a bene viventibus, si dicam nolo, mentior, si dicam volo, timeo, ne sim inanitatis appetentior quam soliditatis. Ergo quid dicam? Nec plene volo nec plene nolo. Non plene volo, ne in laude humana pericliter; non plene nolo, ne ingrati sint, quibus praedico. Cf. also *Enarr. in Ps.* 50. 1; *Serm.* 154. 1. On the custom of applauding preachers in the early Church, cf. J. Zellinger, "Der Beifall in der altchristlichen Predigt," *Festgabe A. Knoepfler* (Freiburg i. Br. 1917) 403-15.

The lines following in the text are bracketed because they are not found in many of the manuscripts, including the one recently collated by A. Souter (cf. above, at end of Introduction).

[105] It is clear from this passage that there was no definite season or time of day set apart for these instructions. The catechist might be interrupted in his work at any time and asked to catechize. If these instructions were to be given to one or only a few, the catechist invited them into his own dwelling. But if he had "a class," and particularly, if at the end of the instruction the candidates were to be admitted solemnly to the catechumenate (cf. Ch. 26 n. 314), the vestibule of the church was most probably used (cf. Ch. 1 n. 7); cf. A. Mayer, *Geschichte des Katechumenats und der Katechese* (Kempten 1886) 271; W. Roetzer, *Des hl. Augustinus Schriften als liturgiegeschichtliche Quelle* (Munich 1930) 225 f.

[106] 2 Cor. 9. 7.

[107] 1 Peter 2. 21.

[108] Cf. Phil. 2. 6-8. The omission and abbreviation *etc.* may be the work of some scribe.

[109] Cf. 1 Cor. 9. 22.

[110] Cf. 2 Cor. 5. 13 f. Various interpretations have been given to *mente excedimus* ("whether we be transported in mind"). Augustine (who reads *excessimus* for *excedimus*) when referring to it always takes it in the meaning of ecstasy. For the following, cf. 2 Cor. 12. 15.

[111] Cf. 1 Thess. 2. 7.

[112] This seems to be a reminiscence of Cicero, *De orat.* 2. 162: Ego autem, si quem nunc plane rudem institui ad dicendum velim, his potius tradam adsiduis uno opere eandem incudem diem noctemque tundentibus, *qui omnis tenuissimas particulas atque omnia minima mansa ut nutrices infantibus pueris in os inserant.* Quintilian has likewise borrowed this comparison: *Inst. orat.* 10. 1. 19; cf. also Gellius 4. 1. 11.

[113] The comparison of the hen is taken from Christ's lament over Jerusalem, Matt. 23. 37. Cf. also Augustine, *Enarr. in Ps.* 58. 10; *In Ioan. Ev. tract.* 15. 7. Augustine, as a keen psychologist, took a great interest in natural phenomena; his powers of observation were remarkable. This instinctive interest in nature may have been stimulated by the reading of Vergil. In the present passage the phrase *teneros fetus* ("her tender brood") is reminiscent of Vergil: *Ecl.* 1. 21; so is *confracta voce* ("with tired cry"): *Aen.* 3. 556. In his emotional passages particularly, Augustine shows the deep and permanent influence of the Roman poet. Vergil had given to the hard, legal Latin language its vocabulary of emotion and pathos; and no one knew and appreciated as did Augustine the magic and allurement and subtle connotation of Vergilian phrases. Cf. the discriminating study by K. H. Schelkle, *Vergil in der Deutung Augustins* (Stuttgart 1939).

[114] From various remarks of Augustine scattered through the treatise it is evident that the instruction given to the *rudes* was informal and that the catechist had full liberty in the choice of subject matter. That the subject matter of the instructions given to the catechumens proper likewise varied, is evident from this passage. For if there were a special instruction for catechumens proper, Augustine need only to have referred the *rudis* to it, for the correction of his erroneous opinions. Again, in Ch. 26. 50, Augustine tells the prospective catechumen what his attitude should be if he hears anything in the Scriptures that he does not understand. Now

if there were a set treatise for the catechumenate, Augustine would simply have had to refer the prospective catechumen to it for a solution of his Scripture difficulties.

[115] Rom. 1. 29 f.

[116] Rom. 2. 4.

[117] Rom. 2. 5.

[118] John 6. 68.

[119] A conflation of John 17. 12 and 1 John 2. 19.

[120] 2 Tim. 2. 19.

[121] Rom. 8. 28. Here the Vulgate version reads: Scimus autem quoniam diligentibus Deum *omnia cooperantur in bonum*; the Old Latin version, *omnia procedunt in bonis*. Most probably Augustine's use of *concurrent in bonum* here is not a slip of the memory but is the reading of some other Old Latin version; for Ambrose, *Hex.* 1. 6, has *omnia concurrunt in bonum*.

[122] The teleological argument for the existence of God. Cf. Ps. 19. 1; Isa. 42. 5; Job 12. 9; Wisd. 1. 13; Rom. 1. 20: Invisibilia enim ipsius, a creatura mundi per ea quae facta sunt, intellecta, conspiciuntur; Aristotle, *De mundo* 6; Philo, *De praem. et poen.* 7. For the Stoic proof of the existence of God, cf. Cicero, *De nat. deor.* 2. 15; *ibid.* 2. 4; *Tusc.* 1. 70; *De leg.* 1. 8. Representative of the Fathers are Tertullian, *Apol.* 17; Athenagoras 4; Minucius Felix, *Oct.* 17. 4; Lactantius, *Inst. div.* 1. 2. 5.

[123] In this chapter we recognize Augustine's two great virtues: a burning love of God and an all-embracing love of his fellow men, whose feelings he has analyzed better perhaps than any writer before his time or since. Augustine throughout this treatise exhibits himself as possessing what Newman (*Historical Sketches* 2. 286) ascribes to St. John Chrysostom, "a versatile recognition of men."

[124] Augustine himself tells us that before his conversion he was drawn to St. Ambrose not so much by the latter's teaching, as because he saw in Ambrose a fellow creature who was kind to him. Cf. *Conf.* 5. 13. 23: Et eum amare coepi primo quidem *non tamquam doctorem veri*, quod in ecclesia tua prorsus desperabam, *sed tamquam hominem benignum in me*.

[125] Augustine employed the acroamatic or lecture method in catechizing. This method was, of course, best adapted for the *narratio*. However, from time to time during the *narratio* he made use of the erotematic or question-and-answer method, not to impart instruction but to ascertain whether or not the candidate was following him; just as before beginning the *narratio* he interrogated the

prospective candidate. Augustine, therefore, in this treatise combines the acroamatic and the erotematic method: the former he uses to impart the knowledge of Christian doctrine; the latter, to guide him in his choice of subject matter and method of presentation, so that the discourse might be adapted to the capacity and peculiarities of the candidate (cf. Ch. 9. 13). In Ch. 8. 10 he writes: cetera vero secundum regulas doctrinae salutaris . . . *narranda vel disserenda sunt;* the catechist must judge for himself whether the instruction should take the form of a lecture or of a discussion. This is the first treatise on catechesis in which the pedagogical value of suggestive questions (*Hilfsfragen*) is brought out. Of course these questions are not to be confused with the formal questions put to the chatechumen when he made his profession of faith (cf. Ch. 26). Cf. H. J. Holtzmann, " Die Katechese der alten Kirche," *Theologische Abhandlungen C. v. Weizsäcker gewidmet* (Freiburg i. Br. 1892) 108.

¹²⁶ Here the adjective *Catholica* is used alone for *Ecclesia Catholica* (" Catholic Church "). African writers frequently use *Catholica* thus elliptically. Cf. Tertullian, *De praescr.* 30; Cyprian, *Ep.* 49. 2. O. Rottmanner in his classical study " Catholica," *Rev. Bén.* 17 (1900) 1-9 (repr. in *Geistesfrüchte* 74 ff.), has shown that Augustine uses *Catholica* 240 times to designate *Ecclesia Catholica.* To Rottmanner's examples add *Contra Ep. Parmen.* 2. 4. 8 (cf. A. Souter, *Jour. of Theol. Stud.* 11 [1909] 149).

O. R. Vassall-Phillips, *The Work of St. Optatus Bishop of Milevis against the Donatists* (London 1917) 50. n. (a), observes " ἡ καθολικὴ 'Εκκλησία or *Ecclesia Catholica* almost always means, in the Fathers, the Church militant on earth at the time when they wrote. Thus even at the beginning of the second century the word Catholic is used by St. Ignatius (*Ep. ad Smyrn.* 8) for the true Church throughout the world, in contrast with heretical sects. It is also found four times in *The Letter of the Church of Smyrna on the Martyrdom of the holy Polycarp.*"

¹²⁷ As the gift of faith is a grace, Augustine insists on the necessity of praying for the candidate; prayer on the part of the catechist being more important than the actual instruction.

¹²⁸ Augustine's homilies on the Gospel of St. John furnish numerous instances of how he enlivened his discourses from time to time with sallies of wit and humorous allusions.

¹²⁹ In his sermons, likewise, Augustine shows himself solicitous for the bodily comfort of his hearers. Augustine in his day recognized a fact that has been brought out very strikingly by Francis Thompson

in his essay, " Health and Holiness" (*The Works of Francis Thompson* 3 [London 1913] 249-81), namely, that there is a very subtle and intimate connection between the spiritual and the corporal. One reason for Augustine's thoughtfulness and considerateness was the fact that he himself was of a very weak constitution, as appears from his *Confessions*, sermons, and letters; cf. B. Legewie " Die körperliche Konstitution und die Krankheiten Augustins," *Miscellanea Agostiniana* 2 (Rome 1931) 5. 21.

¹³⁰ That is, in the churches of Italy.

¹³¹ In the African Church the office of preaching was reserved strictly to the bishop. By special permission Augustine, while still a *presbyter*, preached in presence of his bishop; cf. Possidius, *Vita Aug.* 5. In Africa it was the custom for the preacher to deliver his sermon sittting; cf. Augustine, *Hom.* 49: ut ego vos non diu teneam, praesertim quia *ego sedens loquor*, vos stando laboratis. Augustine intimates that in Italy both the preacher and the people sat.

¹³² Cf. Luke 10. 39.

¹³³ With this phrase (*cui assistunt angeli*) compare Roman Missal, Preface for the Blessing of Palms: *cui assistunt angeli*. It is interesting to note how many expressions of the Fathers have been incorporated in prayers of the liturgy. Cf. A. Manser, " Ambrosiuszitat in einer Votivmesse,". *Jahrb. f. Liturgiew.* 1 (1921) 82.

¹³⁴ This saying of Augustine's on the necessity of preferring God's will to our own was frequently quoted by mediaeval writers.

¹³⁵ Prov. 19. 21.

¹³⁶ Cf. 1 Cor. 6. 20 and 1 Peter 1. 19.

¹³⁷ In the Old Testament *proselytus = advena, peregrinus*, a resident " stranger" or " foreigner." The word was also applied to a convert from heathenism to the Jewish religion. This meaning is present in both passages in which it occurs in the New Testament: Acts 2. 11; Matt. 23. 15: Vae vobis, scribae et Pharisaei hypocritae, quia circuitis mare et aridam, ut faciatis unum *proselytum*; et cum fuerit factus, facitis eum filium gehennae duplo quam vos. *Gehenna* (" hell "), or Valley of Hinnom, was a place near Jerusalem where children were offered to Melek (or Moloch; cf. 4 Kings 23. 10); hence used by later Jews and in Scripture to designate hell.

¹³⁸ Cf. Ps. 50. 19.

¹³⁹ Cf. Eccli. 3. 33.

¹⁴⁰ Cf. Osee 6. 6.

¹⁴¹ The word *foenum*, " hay," is here used in its ecclesiastical meaning of " concupiscence." Cf. Tertullian, *De res. carn.* 59:

demere *foenum carnis immundae*. This use of *foenum* grew out of
1 Cor. 3. 12.

[142] Cf. Deut. 8. 3; Matt. 4. 4; Luke 4. 4.

[143] Cf. Matt. 25. 26 f.

[144] Rom. 5. 5.

[145] Augustine dictated this treatise. This accounts for a certain amount of careless construction, verbosity, repetition, and other defects of improvisation. This practice of dictating treatises as well as of extempore preaching had a harmful influence on the style of the Fathers.

[146] Catechizing must be accommodated to the mental capacity of the candidate: a sound pedagogical principle. For an instance of how Augustine could adapt the exposition of a subject to the mental capacity of his audience, cf. his highly speculative disquisition on the "Word" in *De Trin.* 1, with a popular explanation of the same subject in *Serm. de Trin.* 52. 18. What Wilfrid Ward writes of Cardinal Newman's insight (cf. *Last Lectures by Wilfrid Ward* [London 1918] 125) applies to Augustine: "His consciousness (while writing) of the living minds with which his words were bringing him into contact was almost like a sixth sense. He was so acutely conscious of the effect of any sentence he wrote on the various minds of different classes of readers that merely objective treatment, which neglects the mentality of the reader or is designed for expert minds all on one plane, was impossible to him." Newman himself writes (*Sermon Notes of John Henry Cardinal Newman* [London 1913] 322): "I cannot determine what I shall lecture on till I know who will come, for the speaker speaks according to the hearers."

[147] The term *secta* here designates "a school of philosophy," whose adherents would be more cultivated than those belonging to "this or that popular error." For *secta* in the meaning of "a school of philosophy," cf. Cicero, *Brut.* 120: qui eorum *philosophorum sectam* secutus es. In the Acts of the Apostles *secta* is used disparagingly (in Tertullus's accusation of St. Paul) to designate the Christian religion (cf. 24. 5: auctorem seditionis *sectae Nazarenorum*; 28. 22: nam de *secta* hac notum est nobis quia ubique contradicitur). Harnack (*Mission und Ausbreitung des Christentums in den ersten drei Jahrhunderten* [4th ed., Leipzig 1924] 1. 422 n. 1) observes that up to the middle of the third century *secta* was employed in a good sense by Christian writers, particularly by St. Cyprian (cf., for example, *De bono pat.* 1: *fidei nostrae secta*) to designate the Christian

community. Beginning, however, with the fourth century, it ceases to be used by the Christian writers when speaking of Christianity. In the present passage it seems to be used somewhat contemptuously.

[148] Cf. 1 Cor. 9. 22.

[149] Cf. Ps. 78. 11 and 24. 18.

[150] Next to Rome in wealth and population ranked Alexandria and Carthage. At Carthage Augustine had received his education (cf. *Conf.* 3. 1); and, though in the celebrated wordplay (*Carthago-sartago*) he described it as a hissing caldron of immorality (*Conf.*, *ibid.*: circumstrepebat me undique sartago flagitiosorum amorum), of it he was extremely proud. Cf. his *Ep.* 43. 7: civitas ampla et illustris . . . fama celeberrima nobilis; *Ep.* 118. 10: duae tantum urbes, Latinarum linguarum artifices, Roma atque Carthago. Cf. especially G. G. Lapeyre, " Saint Augustin et Carthage," *Miscellanea Agostiniana* 2 (Rome 1931) 91-148.

[151] Augustine has *Deo gratias*, elliptical for *Deo gratias agamus*: a liturgical formula and likewise a favorite form of salutation in the early Church. Cf. 1 Cor. 15. 57: *Deo* autem *gratias*, qui dedit nobis victoriam; 2 Cor. 2. 14. In Africa it was employed by the Catholics; the Donatists having their own formula, *Deo laudes*. Cf. Augustine, *Enarr. in Ps.* 132. 6.

[152] Too many of Augustine's rhetorical devices are lost in translation. Here he uses the figure of oxymoron: volunt . . . *requiescere in* rebus *inquietis* = " They wish to be at *rest* amid *restless* things." The inability of the soul to be satisfied with the fleeting things of time is a favorite theme with Augustine. Cf. *Conf.* 1. 1. 1 (note again the oxymoron!): quia fecisti nos ad te et *inquietum* est cor nostrum, donec *requiescat* in te.

[153] That a man must leave his riches behind him at death is a literary commonplace. Cf. the famous lines in Horace. *Carm.* 2. 14. 21 ff.:

> Linquenda tellus et domus et placens
> Uxor, neque harum quas colis arborum
> Te praeter invisas cupressos
> Ulla brevem dominum sequetur.

[154] That even the longest life is short is a favorite theme of the Scriptures and of the pagan philosophers. Cf. Job 7. 7: Memento quia ventus est vita mea; and Cicero *Tusc.* 1. 94: Quae vero aetas longa est, aut quid omnino homini longum? For the idea in the following sentence, cf. Terence, *Phorm.* 575: Senectus ipsa est morbus; Seneca, *Ep.* 108. 28: Senectus enim insanabilis morbus est.

[155] Cf. Isa. 40. 6-8.

[156] *Pompae* is often used in ecclesiastical language of the vain show of the world and of the devil. Cf. H. Rahner, "*Pompa diaboli.* Ein Beitrag zur Bedeutungsgeschichte des Wortes πομπή in der nachchristlichen Taufliturgie," *Zeitschr. f. kath. Theol.* 55 (1931) 239-73.

[157] Augustine never tires inveighing against the capital vices of his age, which were gluttony, lust, and a mad craving for theatrical spectacles and gladiatorial combats. For an interesting account of the efforts made by the early Fathers to combat these vices inherited from paganism, cf. E. Bickel, "Das asketische Ideal bei Ambrosius, Hieronymus u. Augustinus," *Neue Jahrb. f. d.* klass. *Altertumswissenschaft* 37 (1916) 437-74.

[158] The meaning of this word is unknown. W. Y. Fausset, *De Catechizandis Rudibus* (3d ed., London 1915), would derive it from σίντης (= "tearing," "ravenous," "devouring"), in Homer an epithet of lions. From the context it must refer to such as maul and maim each other, that is, to gladiators. The phrase *qui appellantur* shows that it was a colloquialism.

[159] The word *thymelici* is used here, from θυμέλη, the altar in the centre of the orchestra. As the players both in Rome and Carthage were for the most part Greeks, the Latin stage vocabulary was filled with Greek words having Latin endings. Apuleius in *Apol.* 13. 416, speaks of the *choragium, thymelicum,* and *syrma.*

[160] The Carthaginians were passionately fond of chariot races. "Factions" with party colors encouraged their favorite charioteers. On the frenzy and passion of these "factions," cf. Tertullian, *De spect.* 23: An Deo placebit *auriga ille tot animarum inquietator, tot furiarum minister?* Cf. J. Köhne, *Die Schrift Tertullians Über die Schauspiele in kultur- und religionsgeschichtlicher Beleuchtung* (diss. Breslau 1929).

[161] Men who were well trained and equipped to fight beasts in the arena, in other words, professionals, were called *venatores,* as here. Criminals who were made to fight beasts were called *bestiarii.*

[162] For a graphic description of the frenzy of the populace at gladiatorial combats, see Augustine, *Conf.* 6. 8. 13: Ut enim vidit illum sanguinem, immanitatem simul ebibit et non se avertit, sed fixit aspectum et hauriebat furias et nesciebat et delectabatur scelere certaminis et cruenta voluptate inebriabatur . . . Spectavit, clamavit, exarsit, abstulit inde secum insaniam. Cf. also Tertullian, *Apol.* 38; Minucius Felix, *Oct.* 37. 11.

[163] Augustine in the *Confessions* 3. 2, discussing why it is that people at stage plays take delight in scenes representing sorrow and misfortune which they themselves would not like to experience, writes: Quid est, quod ibi *homo vult dolere luctuosa et tragica*, quae tamen pati ipse nollet? Et tamen *pati vult ex eis dolorem spectator et dolor ipse est voluptas eius.* Quid est nisi miserabilis insania?

[164] Favorite actors had their rival factions. The jealousies of these factions frequently ended in bloodshed. In this section Augustine touches upon the great vices of the Africans: jealousy, hatred, sensuality, and avarice. On this subject, cf. A. Degert, *Quid ad mores ingeniaque Afrorum cognoscenda conferant Sancti Augustini Sermones* (Paris 1894).

[165] Carthage was, perhaps, the most dissolute city in the Roman Empire. Cf. Salvianus, *De gub. Dei* 7. 17. 24: Unam enim putes fuisse illic libidinum fornicationumque sentinam, caenum quasi ex omni platearum et cloacarum labe collectam: Carthaginem dico . . . ; *ibid.* 16. 66; Quis non omnes omnino Afros generaliter impudicos sciat nisi ad Deum forte conversos . . . ita enim generale in eis malum impuritatis est, ut quicumque ex eis impudicus esse desierit, Afer non esse videatur. Cf. above, n. 150. According to Sallust, *Hist.* 1. 12, greed and luxury increased in Rome after the taking of Carthage.

[166] The immorality of the public baths throughout the Roman Empire was notorious. This was particularly the case in Carthage. Cf. J. Zellinger, *Bad und Bäder in der alten Kirche. Eine Studie über Christentum und Antike* (Munich 1928).

[167] The allusion to fever would be very natural as it was quite prevalent in Roman Africa. It was of fever that Augustine himself died (cf. Possidius, *Vita S. Aug.* 29: *decubuit febribus* fatigatus).

[168] Cf. Prov. 16. 8.

[169] Cf. Matt. 13. 30. This is aimed at the Donatists whose contentions were based mainly on the essential purity of the Church, and as a consequence, on the rigid exclusion of all unworthy members. Augustine, in his writings, emphasizes the fact that the good and the wicked are always to be found together in the Church, but that they are to be separated on the last day.

[170] One of the stock arguments against Christianity was that the God of the Christians did so very little to improve their condition in this world. Cf. Minucius Felix, *Oct.* 12; Tertullian, *Apol.* 41; Lactantius, *Inst. div.* 5. 21. 8: Nam imprimis haec causa est cur existimetur religio Dei vim non habere, quod inducuntur homines

specie terrenorum ac praesentium bonorum, quae ad curam mentis nullo modo pertinent; quibus *quia carere iustos vident, et affluere iniustos, et Dei cultum inanem arbitrantur, in quo inesse illa non cernunt*, et deorum ritus aestimant veros, quoniam cultores eorum et divitiis et honoribus et regnis fruantur; Eusebius, *Hist. Eccles.* 9. 7 f.

[171] For the thought, cf. the hymn, the original of which was a Spanish sonnet mistakenly attributed to St. Francis Xavier:

> O Deus, ego amo te
> Nec amo te, ut salves me
> Aut quia non amantes te
> Aeterno punis igne . . .

For recent literature on the hymn and a succinct discussion of its authorship, see J. M. Cooper, " An Aspect of Perfect Love of God," *Am. Eccl. Rev.* 115 (1946) 110 f.

[172] 1 Cor. 2. 9. Augustine uses this quotation from St. Paul very effectively in the fine passage in *Conf.* 9. 10. 23, in which he describes his last conversation with Monnica at Ostia: Conloquebamur ergo soli . . . et . . . quaerebamus inter nos . . . qualis futura esset vita aeterna sanctorum, *quam nec oculus vidit nec auris audivit nec in cor hominis ascendit.*

[173] Cf. Gen. 2. 2.

[174] Ps. 32. 9 and 148. 5.

[175] According to the millenarian doctrine, as set forth in the Epistle of St. Barnabas (15. 4), of which Augustine was a champion at the time when he wrote this treatise, there are seven *millennia* or epochs of world history, each lasting a thousand years, corresponding to the seven days of Creation. In the seventh spoch (*septima aetate*) after the destruction of the wicked, Christ with the just shall reign on earth. This doctrine was based on the Apocalypse 14. 8. Later on Augustine abandoned this realistic eschatology, and in *De civ. Dei* 20. 5, interpreted it allegorically.

The division of the history of the world into six epochs corresponding to the six days of creation is much older than Augustine. It was known to the authors of the Septuagint and was so firmly rooted in Jewish traditions that it found its way into the Talmud. Among Greek Christian writers besides Barnabas who is the first to mention this chronological system, cf. also Irenaeus, *Adv. haer.* 5. 28. 3; Hippolytus, *Com. in Dan.* 4. 23. 6. Cyprian is the first among Latin Christian writers who speaks of the six ages. Cf. *Ad Fortunatum, praef.* 2: Sex millia annorum iam paene complentur, ex quo hominem diabolus impugnat; cf. also Lactantius, *Inst. div.* 7. 14. 9; Ambrose, *Expos. Ev. sec. Luc.* 7. 7; Jerome, *Ep.* 140. 8. Augustine does not insist upon this division, but simply mentions it as a known fact to all who have attended catechetical lectures.* According to F. Hipler (*Die christliche Geschichtsauffassung* [Cologne 1884] 26), it was most probably at catechetical instructions that Augustine himself first learned of this chronological division of history. However, though this system is not original with Augustine, it was his influence that made it popular, so that in the Middle Ages the division of world history into six epochs became classical. Cf. Isidore of Seville, *Liber etym.* 1. 5. 38; Bede, *De temp.* 16-22. Bonaventure (*Illum. Eccl. in Hexaem.* 15) writes: Notandum est, quod *sicut Deus sex diebus mundum fecit . . . ita corpus Christi mysticum sex habet aetates.* It may be noted here also that the Roman historians were accustomed to divide history into epochs. Lactantius (*Inst. div.* 7. 15. 14) writes: Non inscite Seneca Romanae urbis *tempora distribuit in aetates*; cf. also Florus, *Epit. de T. Liv.* 1. 1; Ammianus Marcellinus 14. 6. 4. Cf. below, n. 250.

[176] Cf. Rom. 8. 30 and Ps. 24. 18

[177] Cf. John 1. 1. The expression *in sancto silentio* ("in holy silence") is reminiscent of Platonism and particularly of Neo-Platonism as represented by Plotinus. Cf. O. Casel, *De philosophorum graecorum silentio mystico* (Giessen 1919); "Vom heiligen Schweigen," *Ben. Monatsschr.* 3 (1921) 417 ff.; G. Mensching, *Das heilige Schweigen* (Giessen 1926).

[178] The Fathers are fond of using *mundare* in its metaphorical meaning of "cleansing from sin." Cf. Ambrose, *De Iacob.* 1. 5. 17: ut totus mundus eius *mundaretur* sanguine; *De patr.* 4. 24: (Christus) nostra, quae fecimus, peccata *mundavit; De off.* 3. 18. 103.

[179] John 3. 16.

[180] Cf. Gen. 1. 31.

[181] Cf. Gen. 1. 26.

[182] Through reason man can come to a knowledge of God; its possession makes him superior to the brute creation. Cf. above, n. 122. See also Cicero, *De nat. deor.* 2. 55: Earum autem (stellarum) perennes cursus atque perpetui . . . declarant in his vim et mentem esse divinam, ut haec ipsa qui non sentiat deorum vim habere, is nihil omnino sensurus esse videtur; cf. Minucius Felix, *Oct.* 17, qui hunc mundi totius ornatum non divina ratione perfectum volunt . . . mentem, sensum, oculos denique ipsos non habere.

For the thought that it is reason that makes man superior to the beast, cf. again Cicero, *De leg.* 1. 30: *ratio qua una praestamus beluis; De nat. deor.* 2. 133: Quorum igitur causa quis dixerit effectum esse mundum? Eorum scilicet animantium, quae ratione utuntur. Hi sunt dii et homines, quibus profecto nihil est melius; *ratio est enim, quae praestet omnibus.*

[183] Cf. Gen. 2. 18. In *De Gen. c. Man.*, written in 388-391, Augustine held that, before the fall, the union of Adam and Eve in matrimony was purely spiritual. Cf. *ibid.* 1. 30: Rectissime quaeritur quemadmodum accipienda sit coniunctio masculi et feminae ante peccatum . . . utrum carnaliter, an spiritualiter accipienda sit. *Licet enim nobis eam etiam spiritualiter accipere,* ut in carnalem fecunditatem post peccatum conversa esse credatur; *ibid.* 2. 15: *et facta dicitur (femina) in adiutorium viri, ut copulatione spirituali spirituales fetus ederet.* He was still of this opinion when he wrote *De cat. rud.* (405), though in *De bono coni.* (401) he had begun to waver. Cf. *De bono coni.* 2: *Nec nunc opus est ut scrutemur, et in ea quaestione definitam sententiam proferamus, unde primorum hominum proles posset existere, quos benedixerat Deus, dicens, crescite et multiplicamini et implete terram, si non peccassent;* cum mortis conditionem corpora eorum peccando meruerint, nec esse concubitus nisi mortalium corporum possit. . . . He revised and definitely stated his opinion in *De Gen. ad litt.* (401-415) 9.5: *Si autem quaeritur, ad quam rem fieri oportuerit hoc adiutorium, nihil aliud probabiliter occurrit, quam propter filios procreandos,* sicut adiutorium semini terra est, ut virgultum ex utroque nascatur; cf. *ibid.* 9. 6, 8, 9, 12; *Retract.* 1. 10. 2. For an exhaustive study of Augustine's doctrine on matrimony, cf. J. Mausbach, *Die Ethik des hl. Augustinus* (2d ed., Freiburg i. Br. 1929) 1. 318 ff.

[184] Cf. 1 Cor. 11. 7-9.

[185] In all his controversies on free will, grace, and the origin of evil, Augustine insists on the superiority of man, even though a sinner, over the beasts of the field; this superiority consists in the possession of reason. Cf. Augustine, *De Gen. ad litt.* 9. 14: Neque enim tantum depravati sunt homines, ut non etiam tales pecoribus et volatilibus antecellant; cf. Luke 12. 24: quanto magis vos pluris estis illis?

[186] Cf. Ps. 144. 3.

[187] Augustine is here referring to the sacrament of penance without mentioning it directly.

[188] Augustine here touches upon the momentous question of predestination upon which he was to write so much later on in the

Pelagian controversy. Cf. Augustine, *De Gen. ad litt.* 11.6: *Cum etiam per iniustos iusti ac per impios pii proficiunt, frustra dicitur: Non crearet Deus, quos praesciebat malos futuros. Cur enim non crearet, quos praesciebat bonis profuturos, ut et utiles eorum bonis voluntatibus exercendis admonendisque nascantur et iuste pro sua mala voluntate puniantur?* Recent studies on Augustine and predestination are very numerous; to mention but three: J. Saint-Martin, *La pensée de s. Augustin sur la prédestination gratuite et infallible des élus à la gloire d'après ses derniers écrits, 426/7–430* (Paris 1930); A. M. Jacquin, "La prédestination d'après s. Augustin," *Miscellanea Agostiniana* 2 (Rome 1931) 853-78; F. Cayré, "La prédestination dans s. Augustin," *Année théol.* 2 (1941) 42-63.

[189] Though God is not the author of sin, yet He can make the sinner conform to the divine order (*cadentem ordinat*) by the justice of His punishments. Cf. Augustine, *Conf.* 1.10.6; also *Enarr. in Ps.* 8.15; *De Gen. ad litt.* 3.24.37; *De cat. rud.* in this section, below: "For God knows how to make souls that forsake him conform ..."; *De mus.* 7.11; *C. Faust.* 16.21.

[190] *Liberum arbitrium* is a consecrated phrase among theologians to designate "free will." For the expression, cf. Lactantius, *Inst. div.* 2.8.4; Jerome, *Adv. Pelag.* 3.7. Augustine wrote two treatises on free will: *De libero arbitrio* (388) and *De gratia et libero arbitrio* (426).

[191] There were three main reasons adduced in the early Church for the fall of the angels: 1) that they fell through *lust*, being enamored of the daughters of men: cf. Gen. 6.1 ff.; Enoch 6; Justin, *Apol.* 2.5; Athenagoras 24; Tertullian, *De cult. fem.* 1; 2) that they fell through *envy* of man, whom God had created: cf. Irenaeus, *Adv. haer.* 4.40.3; Cyprian, *De zelo et livore* 4; 3) that they fell through *pride*; this was the theory most commonly accepted in Augustine's time: cf. Eusebius, *Praep. ev.* 7.16; Athanasius, *De virg.* 5; Cyril of Jerusalem, *Cat.* 2.3; Gregory of Nazianzus, *Arc.* 6.

[192] Augustine may have in mind here the Manichaean theory according to which the principle of evil could harm the principle of good.

[193] Though the number of the wicked is greater than the number of the just, even as there is more chaff than grain, still, relatively speaking, the number of the just is great. Cf. Augustine, *De unit. Eccl.* 14.36: *multi per se ipsos considerati, pauci autem in comparatione iniquorum.* Cf. Matt. 7.3.

[194] We must not make the mistake of translating *civitas* here by

"state." *Civitas* is here used by Augustine in the meaning of city, society, or organized community with the rights of citizenship, without any reference to a material city. In *De cat. rud.* 21. 37, he makes this plain by using the phrase *civitatem societatemque*. Cf. also *De civ. Dei* 14. 1: Ac per hoc factum est, ut . . . non tamen amplius quam *duo quaedam genera humanae societatis existerent, quae civitates duas* secundum scripturas nostras merito *appellare possemus; ibid.* 15. 18: superna *civitas, id est hominum societas; ibid.* 15. 20: haec terrena *civitas societasque hominum.*

This conception of the word *civitas* is not original with Augustine. In fact it was so familiar to his African hearers (particularly through its use in the Scriptures and in Tyconius) that Augustine employs it without a word of explanation. *Civitas* in its Augustinian sense can be traced back to Plato. Cf. *Leg.* 713 A.; 731 E.; *Rep.* 592 B. We have likewise the authority of Clement of Alexandria that it was used by the Stoics in this meaning (*Strom.* 4. 26. 172. 2 f.). It is likewise found in its Augustinian sense in Latin authors. Cf. Cicero, *De leg.* 1. 23: ut iam universus hic mundus *una civitas communis deorum atque hominum* existimanda sit; also Seneca, *De otio* 4. 1. The Scriptures, of course, had familiarized the Christians with the notion of the *civitas.* Cf. Ps. 86. 3: Gloriosa dicta sunt de te, *civitas Dei*; Ps. 47. 2; Magnus Dominus, et laudabilis nimis in *civitate Dei* nostri; Heb. 11. 10: Expectabat enim fundamenta habentem *civitatem, cuius artifex et conditor Deus; ibid.* 12. 22: Sed accessistis ad Sion montem, et *civitatem Dei viventis, Ierusalem caelestem*; Apoc. 3. 12: Et scribam super eum nomen Dei mei, et nomen *civitatis Dei mei novae Ierusalem; ibid.* 21. 2: Et ego Ioannes vidi *sanctam civitatem Ierusalem novam.* Tyconius, whose exegetical skill was highly esteemed by Augustine, likewise greatly influenced him. Cf. Tyconius, *Comm. in Apocalypsin* (the text as reconstructed by T. Hahn in his *Tyconius-Studien* [Stud. z. Gesch. d. Theol. u. d. Kirche 6. 2, Leipzig 1900]) 25: Ecce, *duas civitates, unam Dei et unam diaboli; ibid.* 29: Perspicue patet *duas civitates esse et duo regna et duos reges, Christum et diabolum*: et ambo super *utrasque civitates* regnant . . . *hae duae civitates, una mundo et una desiderat servire Christo* . . . hae utraeque ita laborant in unum, una ut habeat unde damnetur, altera ut habeat unde salvetur.

Augustine makes his first reference to these two rival communities in *De vera rel.* (written about 390) 25, without, however, using the word *civitas: Universum genus humanum* ab Adam usque ad finem huius saeculi, ita sub divinae providentiae legibus administratur, ut *in duo genera distributum* appareat. Quorum *in uno est turba impiorum*, terreni hominis imaginem ab initio saeculi usque ad finem gerentium. *In altero series populi uni Deo dediti*, sed ab Adam usque ad Ioannem Baptistam terreni hominis vitam gerentis servili quadam iustitia. He applies the term *civitates* to the two rival communities for the first time in the present passage of our treatise. The idea of comparing these two communities to two cities was suggested, most probably, by the *Rules* of Tyconius in which the famous Donatist exegete speaks of the two cities, the one of God, the other of the devil. This contrast of the two cities was later on to form the central theme of Augustine's great work, *De civitate Dei*. Cf. *De civ. Dei* 14. 28: Fecerunt itaque *civitates duas* amores duo, *terrenam* scilicet amor sui usque ad contemptum Dei, *caelestem* vero amor Dei usque ad contemptum sui; cf. also *ibid*. 15. 1: Quod (genus hominum) in duo genera distribuimus, unum eorum, qui secundum hominem, alterum eorum, qui secundum Deum vivunt; *quas etiam mystice appellamus civitates duas*. Cf. H. Hermelink, "Die *civitas terrena* bei Augustin," *Festgabe für A. von Harnack* (Tübingen 1921) 302-24. See also O. Schilling, *Die Staats- und Soziallehre des hl. Augustinus* (Freiburg i. Br. 1910); C. Butti, *La mente di S. Agostino nella Città di Dio* (Florence 1930); V. J. Bourke, *Augustine's Quest of Wisdom* (Milwaukee 1945) Ch. 13: "God and Society," 248-84.

[195] Sin is frequently likened in ecclesiastical language to a weight (*pondus*); cf. Roman Missal, Collect for the Feast of S. Gregory the Great: qui *peccatorum* nostrorum *pondere* premimur; cf. Augustine, *De civ. Dei* 1. 28; Prudentius, *Cath*. 10. 27. The metaphor may have been suggested by Wisd. 9. 15: *Corpus* enim, quod corrumpitur, *aggravat animam*, et *terrena inhabitatio deprimit sensum* multa cogitantem.

[196] Cf. Gen. 6 f.

[197] Cf. Jonas 3.

[198] The deluge was a symbol of the sacrament of baptism. Cf. 1 Peter 3. 20: Cum fabricaretur arca, in qua pauci, id est octo animae salvae factae sunt per aquam: quod et *vos nunc similis formae salvos facit baptisma*. For further patristic references to the deluge as a symbol of baptism, see J. Quasten, *Monumenta eucharistica et liturgica vetustissima* (Bonn 1935-37) 118 and 145.

[199] The wood of the Ark by which Noe and his family were saved is a figure of the Cross. Cf. Gal. 3. 13: *Christus* nos redemit de maledicto legis, *factus pro nobis maledictum: quia scriptum est: Maledictus omnis qui pendet in ligno*.

[200] It is bad enough to adore what God made; cf. Rom. 1. 25: *qui commutaverunt veritatem Dei in mendacium, et coluerunt et servierunt creaturae potius quam creatori*. It is still worse to adore what has been made by man; Acts 17. 29: *Genus ergo cum simus Dei, non debemus aestimare auro, aut argento, aut lapidi, sculpturae artis, et cogitationis hominis, divinum esse simile*. All the apologists point out the stupidity and blindness of the pagans in adoring their own handiwork. Cf. Minucius Felix, *Oct.* 22: *Quis ergo dubitat horum imagines consecratas vulgus orare et publice colere, dum opinio et mens imperitorum artis concinnitate decipitur . . . ecce funditur, fabricatur, sculpitur: nondum deus est . . . tunc postremo deus est, cum homo illum voluit et dedicavit*; cf. Tertullian, *Apol.* 12. Even pagan writers saw the absurdity of "making" gods. Cf. Martial, *Ep.* 8. 24. 5:

> Qui fingit sacros auro vel marmore vultus
> Non facit ille deos: qui rogat, ille facit.

[201] For the distinction in the use of these terms, cf. the phrase of the Fourth Lateran Council, *diabolus enim et alii daemones*: that is, by *diabolus* is meant Satan himself, while the rest of the fallen angels, his subordinates, are called *daemones* or *daemonia*. Cf. E. Schneweis, *Angels and Demons according to Lactantius* (Stud. in Christ. Ant. 3, Washington 1944) 105-109.

[202] The idea that worship paid to false gods was in reality paid to demons was common among the Jews, from whom it easily passed into the early Christian writers. Cf. 1 Cor. 10. 20: *Sed quae immolant gentes, daemoniis immolant, et non deo*. Cf. also Tertullian, *De idol.* 4; Augustine, *De civ. Dei* 2. 24. 1: *Nempe (dii) intelleguntur daemones*, sicut saepe dixi notumque nobis est in litteris sacris . . . . Cf. G. Bareille, "Angélologie d'après les Pères," *Dict. de théol. cath.* 1. 2 (1905) 1191-222; also E. Mangenot, "Démon d'après les Pères," *ibid.* 4. 1 (1911) 339-84. Many of the early Christian writers believed that pagan cult statues were tenanted by demons, who took for themselves the worship meant for the gods. Cf. Cyprian, *Quod idola dii non sint* 7: *Hi ergo spiritus sub statuis atque imaginibus consecratis delitescunt*; *Passio S. Symphorosae* 1 (23 Ruinart): *sacrificiis idolorum ac daemonum qui in idolis habitant*; Minucius Felix, *Oct.* 27: *Isti igitur impuri spiritus daemones*, ut ostensum magis a philosophis et a Platone, *sub statuis et imaginibus consecratis delitescunt*; Tertullian, *Apol.* 21; Lactantius, *Inst. div.* 2. 14. 13.

[203] There were indeed just men in the Old Testament, but they were justified by the future merits of Jesus Christ.

[204] For the expression, cf. Apoc. 21. 2: Et ego Ioannes vidi *sanctam civitatem* Ierusalem novam, descendentem de caelo; also *ibid.* 17. 12.

[205] Cf. Gen. 12 ff. The history of Abraham and of the promises made to him is set forth at great length in Book 16 of the *De civitate Dei.*

[206] *Sacramentum Filii Dei*: "the mystery or revelation, concerning the Son of God." Cf. Eph. 1. 9: ut notum faceret nobis *sacramentum* voluntatis suae, where *sacramentum* translates μυστήριον. In Biblical Greek, however, μυστήριον does not mean a mystery, as the word is commonly used in English, but "a truth once hidden, and now revealed"—a revelation. The word μυστήριον occurs 21 times in St. Paul; it has been translated indiscriminately as *sacramentum* and *mysterium.* "The mystery," of course, referred to here, is the Incarnation of the Second Person of the Blessed Trinity. Sometimes, too, in this treatise Augustine refers to the mystery of the Incarnation as *humilitas* ("humility" *par excellence*). Cf. the preceding sentence in this section. Augustine, when using this word to designate the Incarnation, had in mind Phil. 2. 8: *Humiliavit semetipsum factus obediens usque ad mortem*; this is one of his favorite texts.

[207] Cf. Gal. 3. 7.

[208] Ps. 123. 8.

[209] Cf. the Athanasian Creed—also known as the *Quicumque*—in which each Person of the Blessed Trinity is said to have: *aequalis* gloria, *coaeterna* maiestas. Owing to the Christological heresies of the fifth century it became necessary to define dogmatic truths with greater precision. To this end many new compound adjectives such as *consubstantialis, coaeternus,* were coined.

[210] Cf. the Nicene Creed: *qui propter nos* homines . . . et *homo factus est.*

[211] Cf. Col. 1. 18: Et ipse est *caput corporis ecclesiae;* 1 Cor. 12. 12: Sicut enim *corpus unum est, et membra habet multa,* omnia autem membra corporis cum sint multa, unum tamen corpus sunt: ita et Christus. Augustine is ever an exponent of the doctrine of the Mystical Body of Christ: cf. E. Mersch, *Le corps mystique du Christ* (2d ed., Brussels 1936) 2. 35-138; S. J. Grabowski, "St. Augustine and the Doctrine of the Mystical Body of Christ," *Theol. Stud.* 7 (1946) 72-125.

[212] Augustine always teaches that the Saints of the Old Testament were Christians through their faith in Christ who was to come. They were of "the primitive Church," *ecclesia primitivorum,* ἐκκλησία πρωτοτόκων; cf. Heb. 12. 23; Ps.—Clement, *Ad Cor.* 14. 1-4.

"The difficult problem of the concept of the 'pre-existent Church'
. . . still needs to be investigated comprehensively": cf. J. C.
Plumpe, *Mater Ecclesia* (Washington 1943) 23 (see *ibid.* n. 17 for
references in recent works).

²¹³ Cf. Exod. 1. 8 ff.

²¹⁴ Cf. F. J. Dölger, "Der Durchzug durch das Rote Meer als
Sinnbild der christlichen Taufe," *Antike und Christentum* 2 (1930)
63-69; for the deluge as such a symbol, see above, n. 198.

Three Latin forms for baptism occur, *baptismus, baptisma (-atis)*,
and *baptismum*, as here, which form, however, is relatively rare.
It occurs in the Old Latin version, Matt. 21. 25: *baptismus* Ioannis
unde erat. Augustine most probably had the Old Latin version form
in mind here. Baptism is the only sacrament referred to explicitly in
this treatise; but note how he prepares the ground for, and skillfully
leads up to, the other sacraments.

²¹⁵ Cf. Rom. 6. 4: Consepulti enim sumus cum illo *per baptismum*
in mortem: ut quomodo Christus surrexit a mortuis per gloriam
Patris, ita et nos *in novitate vitae* ambulemus.

²¹⁶ Cf. Exod. 12. 3 ff.

²¹⁷ Cf. Isa. 53. 7.

²¹⁸ Just as the Israelites marked their doorposts with the blood of
a lamb, so the catechumens are signed with the Cross, the symbol
of Christ's Passion and death. The signing of the forehead was one
of the ceremonies attending initiation into the catechumenate (cf.
Ch. 8 and n. 87). Cf. Augustine, *Enarr. in Ps.* 141. 9: *Usque adeo
de cruce non erubesco,* ut non in occulto loco habeam crucem Christi,
sed *in fronte portem; Serm.* 215. 5: Denique ne dubitares, ne
erubesceres, *quando primum credidisti, signum Christi in fronte*
tamquam in domo pudoris *accepisti.* The catechumens who were
about to receive baptism were likewise signed upon the forehead.
Cf. *Rituale Romanum, Ordo Baptismi: Accipe signum crucis tam in
fronte, quam in corde.* Cf. B. Busch, *De initiatione christiana secundum doctrinam S. Augustini inquisitio liturgico-historica,* (Rome
1939).

²¹⁹ Augustine by *legem* here means the Decalogue which he simply
mentions without making any attempt to explain it, since he takes it
for granted that the candidates are already familiar with it.—"Written by the finger of God": cf. Exod. 8. 19; 31. 18; Deut. 9. 10;
Ps. 8. 4.

²²⁰ Augustine is here referring to Matt. 12. 28: Si autem ego *in
spiritu Dei eicio daemones;* and Luke 11. 20: Porro si *in digito Dei*

eicio daemonia. From a comparison of these two texts, together with the passages cited above from the Old Testament, it may easily be seen how *digitus Dei* came to be identified with *Spiritus Dei*; cf. Augustine, *De spir. et litt.* 16. 28: *Hic Spiritus Sanctus, per quem diffunditur caritas in cordibus vestris, quae plentitudo legis est, etiam digitus Dei in Evangelio dicitur;* cf. also Ambrose, *In Ps.* 118. 15. 9: *Digitum enim pro Spiritu legimus, ut lex digito Dei scripta est; De Spir. Sanct.* 3. 2. 13. The "finger of God" is likewise identified with the Holy Spirit by Irenaeus, *Dem. praed. apost.* 26: "And in the wilderness Moses received the Law from God, the Ten Words on tables of stone, written with the finger of God (now the finger of God is that which is stretched forth from the Father in the Holy Spirit); and the commandments and ordinances which he delivered to the children of Israel to observe." The allegorical method of exegesis was, therefore, a powerful weapon against the Manichaeans, for it struck at literalism upon which most of the Manichaean objections, particularly to the Old Testament, were based. For Augustine's account of Manichaean literalism and of the allegorical method of St. Ambrose, cf. *Conf.* 5. 14. 24.

[221] This is aimed at the Manichaeans, who were accustomed to cite such texts as Exod. 31. 18: Deditque dominus . . . duas tabulas testimonii lapideas, *scriptas digito Dei*; and Deut. 9. 10: Deditque mihi Dominus duas tabulas lapideas *scriptas digito Dei*—to prove that the orthodox conception of God was anthropomorphic (cf. Augustine, *Conf.* 3. 7. 12). Augustine interpreted these texts allegorically; cf. *Ep.* 148. 13: *Nam de membris Dei, quae assidue Scriptura commemorat, ne quisquam secundum carnis huius formam et figuram nos esse crederet similes Deo*, propterea eadem Scriptura et alas habere Deum dixit, quas utique non habemus. Sicut ergo alas cum audimus, protectionem intelligimus: sic et cum audimus manus, operationem intelligere debemus . . . *et si quid aliud eadem Scriptura tale commemorat, puto spiritualiter intelligendum.*

[222] The Holy Ghost is referred to in Scripture as *donum Dei*; cf. John 4. 10: Si scires *donum Dei*; Acts 2. 38: Et accipietis *donum Spiritus Sancti*; ibid. 20: Pecunia tua tecum sit in perditionem: quoniam *donum Dei* existimasti pecunia possideri; also Augustine, *De cat. rud.* 27. 55: Quam non implet, nisi qui *donum* acceperit *Spiritum Sanctum; Conf.* 13. 9. 10: Cum ergo tantum de *Spiritu Sancto* dictum est hoc . . . de quo solo dictum est, quod sit *donum uum; De Trin.* 15. 18. 32; etc. Cf. also the hymn, *Veni Creator Spiritus* 5 f.: Qui Paraclitus diceris, *Donum Dei* altissimi.

²²³ Cf. Augustine, *Serm.* 156. 14: *Dicitur Spiritus Sanctus digitus Dei propter partitionem donorum,* quae in eo dantur unicuique propria, *in nullis enim membris nostris magis apparet partitio quam in digitis.*

²²⁴ Augustine admits that the law was given to Moses on tablets of stone; not, however, to signify that it was a law of servile fear, but to typify the stubbornness of the Jewish people. He is at pains to show that love was the foundation of the Old Law, because the Manichaeans were forever objecting that the Old and New Testament were in contradiction (cf. *C. Faust.* 15. 4). The latter contrasted, for example, the two texts: 2 Cor. 3. 2: Epistula nostra . . . scripta non atramento, sed Spiritu Dei vivi; *non in tabulis lapideis,* sed in tabulis cordis carnalibus, and Exod. 31. 18: Deditque Dominus . . . duas *tabulas testimonii lapideas,* scriptas digito Dei. In refuting this apparent contradiction, Augustine cited from the Old Testament, Ezech. 11. 19: *Auferam eis cor lapideum et dabo eis cor carneum.*

²²⁵ While asserting against the Manichaeans that love was necessary for the fulfilling of the law in the Old Testament (cf. also *Ep.* 177. 10), Augustine, at the same time, does not fail to show that the New Testament was immeasurably superior to the Old because of the grace of Christ, the Redeemer, and of the charity of the Holy Ghost, the Paraclete.

²²⁶ Cf. Heb. 12. 22; Apoc. 3. 12; Gal. 4. 24-26. The earthly Jerusalem in bondage is a figure of the heavenly Jerusalem, which is free.

²²⁷ Augustine knew very little Hebrew. Cf. O. Rottmanner, "Zur Sprachenkenntnis des hl. Augustinus," in *Theol. Quartalschr.* 12 (1895) 269. He would seem to have had some sort of dictionary of Hebrew proper names. His interpretation of the name as *visio pacis,* "vision of peace," has an exact counterpart in Athanasius, *In Ps.* 64. 2: Ἰερουσαλὴμ ἑρμηνεύεται ὅρασις εἰρήνης. Cf. F. X. Wutz, *Onomastica Sacra (Texte u. Unters.* 41, Leipzig 1914) 585. Cf. too, the first line of that fine old hymn: *Urbs beata Ierusalem dicta pacis visio.*

²²⁸ The *civitas caelestis* is composed not only of the blessed in heaven but also of the good who are still pilgrims upon earth. Cf. Augustine, *De civ. Dei* 19. 17: *civitas* autem *caelestis vel* potius *pars eius, quae in hac mortalitate peregrinatur et vivit ex fide.* . . . Augustine is fond of contrasting the pride of the devil with the humility of Christ. The citizens of the earthly city imitate the pride of the devil; the citizens of the city of God, the humility of Christ.

Cf. *De civ. Dei* 9. 20: *Contra superbiam* porro *daemonum*, qua pro meritis possidebatur genus humanum, *Dei hùmilitas, quae in Christo apparuit. . . .*

[229] St. Augustine's regard for Christ as King, again and again expressed in the present treatise, received special recognition when in 1925 the Feast of Christ the King was proclaimed and the lessons (7 and 8) of the Third Nocturn were taken from his *In Ioannis Evangelium tractatus.*

[230] Cf. Rom. 1. 3.

[231] Rom. 9. 5.

[232] The second part of *De doctrina Christiana*, completed shortly before Augustine's death, treats of the method and spirit in which the sense of Scripture should be taught (cf. Introduction, n. 10). It supplements the more special "pedagogics" of the present treatise.

[233] According to Gen. 11. 9: Et idcirco vocatum est nomen eius Babel, quia ibi *confusum est* labium universae terrae—Babylonia is derived from the Hebrew *Bālal*. The common opinion today is that it is derived from the Babylonian *bab-ilu* = gate of God. Note that Augustine does not give this etymology on his own authority: *dicitur interpretari confusio.* This is his usual practice when dealing with Hebrew names. Cf. also *Ep. ad Ianuarium* 55. 10: Iericho appellatur, quae in Hebraeo eloquio luna *interpretari dicitur; De civ. Dei* 16. 4: Babylon quippe *interpretatur* confusio; 16. 10; 16. 11; 16. 17; 17. 16 (cf. Wutz, *Onomast. Sacra* 153).

[234] Cf. Jer. 27.

[235] Cf. Dan. 2. 47, 3. 95 ff., 4. 34 (Nabuchodonosor); 6. 25-27 (Darius).

[236] Cf. Jer. 29. 5 ff.

[237] Cf. Rom. 13. 1.

[238] Cf. Rom. 13. 7.

[239] Christians must obey their temporal rulers except when what is ordered is contrary to the divine law; cf. Augustine, *De lib. arb.* 1. 6. 14; *In Ioan. Ev. tract.* 6. 25; *Ep.* 105. 2. 7; etc. See, too, O. Schilling, *Die Staats- und Soziallehre des hl. Augustinus* (Freiburg i. Br. 1910) 78-82.

[240] Cf. Matt. 17. 27.

[241] Cf. Col. 3. 22; Eph. 6. 5.

[242] Babylon, the "city of confusion," typifies the "confusion" of the world, as Jerusalem typifies the peace of eternal life.

In the following Augustine refers to such emperors as Constantine, who embraced Christianity. Zeal for God's worship is one of the characteristics of the ideal ruler. Cf. Augustine's "mirror of princes" in *De civ. Dei* 5. 24: Sed felices eos dicimus, . . . *si suam potestatem ad Dei cultum maxime dilatandum maiestati eius famulam faciunt*; si Deum timent, diligunt, colunt; cf. also H. Tiralla, *Das augustinische Idealbild der christlichen Obrigkeit* (diss. Greifswald 1916).

²⁴³ Cf. 1 Tim. 2. 1 f. On the Christian practice of praying for those in authority, read Tertullian, *Apol.* 39: *Oramus etiam pro imperatoribus, pro ministris eorum et potestatibus*; Arnobius 4. 36. Cf. L. Biehl, *Das liturgische Gebet für Kaiser und Reich* (Paderborn 1937) 31-33. The custom of praying for the prosperity of the Roman Emperor and Empire can be traced back to the earliest Christian times. Cf. above all Clement of Rome, *Cor.* 60. 4–61. 2, and J. A. Kleist's observations, *ACW* 1. 116 n. 175. It was based on the belief that the preservation and well-being of the Church depended on the strength and safety of the Empire. Augustine insists on this point because the Donatists instead of promoting good relations were forever fomenting trouble between Church and State. Cf. Optatus 3. 3.

Though both the Vulgate and the Old Latin version of 1 Tim. 2. 2 read *castitate* ("chastity"), I prefer to follow the editors here who read *caritate* ("charity"). In all his other works, Augustine, when quoting this text, has *caritate*.

²⁴⁴ The reference in this passage is to Constantine and his successors. Cf. O. Schilling, *Die Staats- und Soziallehre des hl. Augustinus* (Freiburg i. Br. 1910) 8-17: "Die Religionspolitik der christlichen Kaiser."

²⁴⁵ 1 Cor. 3. 9.

²⁴⁶ Cf. Jer. 25. 12 and 29. 10.

²⁴⁷ In 458 B. C., under Artaxerxes I, the political and religious restoration of Judea was brought about by Esdras, its governor. In 332 B. C. Alexander the Great marched against Jerusalem, but was prevailed upon to spare it. After his death the Jews were in constant turmoil, owing to the struggle between the Seleucids of Syria and the Ptolemies of Egypt. In 170 B. C. Antiochus Epiphanes took Jerusalem and plundered it (1 Mac. 1. 17-25; 2 Mac. 5. 11-23). Judas Machabeus, after defeating the Syrians (164 B. C.), entered into an alliance with the Romans (1 Mac. 8). The period from 164 B. C. to 64 B. C. is taken up with constant struggles against the Syrians and finally with civil war between Hyrcanus II and Aristobulus.

²⁴⁸ In 65 B. C., by virtue of the alliance with Rome, Pompey came

from Damascus to Jerusalem to put an end to the civil war. After a siege of three months he finally captured the city, made Hyrcanus high priest, and declared Jerusalem a tributary of Rome. Cf. Josephus, *Antiq. Iud.* 14. 4. 1; *Bell. Iud.* 1. 7. 1.

[249] For the division of all history into six epochs (*aetates*) cf. Augustine, *De civ. Dei* 22. 30; *De Trin.* 4. 7; *Quaest. in Hept.* 7. 49; *Serm.* 259. 2; *Enarr. in Ps.* 92. 1; *In Ioan. Ev. tract.* 9. 6; *ibid., tract.* 15. 9. Cf. below, n. 298.

[250] According to the millenarian doctrine held by Augustine at this time, but later abandoned, there have been from the Creation to the coming of Christ five *millennia* or week days of history (cf. above, n. 175). The period that has elapsed since the coming of Christ constitutes the sixth *aetas*. According to Augustine, the duration of this sixth epoch is uncertain. Cf. *De div. quaest.* 83. 58: aetas ultima generis humani, quae incipit a Domini adventu, usque in finem saeculi quibus generationibus computetur incertum est; cf. also *De Gen. c. Man.* 1. 42; *Serm.* 259. Note, too, the *Martyrologium Romanum* for December 25: *sexta mundi aetate* Iesus Christus . . . natus est.

[251] Note how Augustine allegorizes on the sixth day of Creation and the sixth age of the world. Cf. Augustine, *De Gen. c. Man.* 1. 35; *C. Faust.* 12. 8: Sex diebus in Genesi consummavit Deus omnia opera sua, et septimo requievit. Sex aetatibus humanum genus hoc saeculo per successiones temporum, Dei opera insigniunt: quarum prima est ab Adam usque ad Noe; secunda, a Noe usque ad Abraham; tertia, ab Abraham usque ad David; quarta, a David usque ad transmigrationem in Babyloniam; quinta, inde usque ad humilem adventum Domini nostri Iesu Christi; sexta quae nunc agitur, donec Excelsus veniat ad iudicium; septima vero intellegitur in requie sanctorum. . . . *Sexto die in Genesi formatur homo ad imaginem Dei: sexta aetate saeculi manifestatur reformatio nostra in novitate mentis, secundum imaginem eius qui creavit nos.*

[252] Cf. 1 John 4. 19.

[253] Cf. 1 John 4. 9.

[254] The New Testament typifies the new life of grace. For the allusion in *novum testamentum haereditatis sempiternae,* cf. Heb. 9. 15; also Rom. 6. 4. Note the Pauline phraseology throughout this passage. St. Paul was Augustine's favorite guide and teacher. They had much in common; both had been converted from a life of sin to a life of grace. It was the reading of Rom. 14. 4 (cf. *Conf.* 8. 16. 29) that had decided Augustine to break with the old life of sin, and

embrace the new life of grace. Paul and Augustine are both monuments of the saving grace of the new dispensation.

[255] Cf. Heb. 8. 8-13; Rom. 6. 6.

[256] The word *intellegere* is here used in its Scriptural meaning of "to lay to heart," "to obey the moral law." For this meaning, cf. Matt. 13. 19: qui audit verbum Dei, et *non intellegit*.

[257] The passage that follows is, perhaps, the finest in the treatise. It offers a splendid example of what ancient rhetoric (*De subl.* 11) termed *auxesis* or amplification, whereby the augmented instances rise to a height of great beauty and grandeur.

[258] Cf. Augustine, *Serm.* 51. 18: *Virgo concepit, virgo peperit, virgo permansit; Serm.* 184. 3: *quam virgo ante conceptum, tam virgo post partum; Serm.* 186. 1: *concipiens virgo, pariens virgo, virgo gravida, virgo feta, virgo perpetua; Serm.* 121. 4: *Concipit virgo virilis ignara consortii, . . . impletur uterus nullo humano pollutus amplexu, . . . virgo concipit, virgo gravida, virgo feta, virgo perpetua.* See P. Friedrich, *Die Mariologie des hl. Augustinus* (Cologne 1907) 273; also S. Protin, "La Mariologie de St. Augustin," *Rev. August.* 1 (1902) 374.

[259] Cf. 2 Cor. 8. 9.

[260] Cf. Col. 1. 16.

[261] Cf. John 18. 36.

[262] Augustine is always insisting on the humility of Christ. Cf. *De virg.* 32; 37; *In Ioan. Ev. tract.* 25. 16-19; 55. 7; *Enarr. in Ps.* 93. 15; *De civ. Dei* 14. 13; etc.

[263] The Fathers of the fifth century, following St. Paul (cf. Phil. 2. 7: Sed semetipsum exinanivit formam servi accipiens, *in similitudinem hominum factus, et habitu inventus ut homo*) and St. Ignatius of Antioch (cf. *Ephes.* 7. 2, *Trall.* 9. 1, *Smyrn.* 1 ff.), laid great stress on the reality of Christ's human feelings. Cf. Athanasius, *C. Ar.* 3. 26. 34: Cyril of Jerusalem, *Cat.* 4. 9; Leo, *De pass. Dom., serm.* 63. 4: *Omnes enim infirmitates nostras,* quae veniunt de peccato, absque peccati communione suscepit, *ut famis et sitis, somni et lassitudinis, maeroris ac fletus affectionibus non careret, doloresque saevissimos usque ad mortis extrema pateretur.* The humility of the Creator in becoming man was likewise a favorite theme of the Fathers. Note, too, how skillfully Augustine describes the two natures of Christ by antithesis. This use of antithesis was very common in the catecheses of both the Eastern and Western Church. Cf. F. Probst, *Katechese und Predigt* (Breslau 1884) 71.

[264] Cf. Ezech 18. 7; John 6. 51.

[265] Cf. Apoc. 21. 6; John 4. 14.

[266] Cf. John 4. 6.

[267] Cf. John 14. 6: "I am the way, and the truth, and the life." The idea of Christ making Himself our way to heaven is a favorite one with Augustine; cf. *De doctr. christ.* 1. 11. 11; *De util. cred.* 15. 33. The double function of the Incarnation, namely, that Christ as God is the end of our going while Christ as man is the way we go, is succinctly expressed by Augustine in *De civ. Dei* 11. 2: ut idem ipse sit Deus et homo, *quo itur Deus, qua itur homo.*

[268] Cf. Isa. 53. 7; Matt. 26. 63; Mark 7. 37.

[269] Death has no terrors for such as consider death the end of all. Cf. Wisd. 2. 2; 1 Cor. 15. 32: *Si (secundum hominem) ad bestias pugnavi, quid mihi prodest, si mortusi non resurgunt? Manducemus et bibamus; cras enim moriemur.* The Christian, on the other hand, has a salutary fear of death, not on account of death itself but because of the judgment to follow; cf. Heb. 9. 27. The Resurrection of Christ from the dead is a pledge of the Christian's resurrection; no one can say, therefore, that he has learned from Christ to despise death as though destined never to live again. Cf. A. C. Rush, *Death and Burial in Christian Antiquity* (Stud. in Christ. Ant. 1, Washington 1941) 1-72.

[270] Cf. Acts 1. 3. 9.

[271] Cf. Acts 2. Augustine here shows how, through the descent of the Holy Ghost upon the Apostles on the feast of Pentecost, the Decalogue was promulgated a second time; this time however it was a law of love and not, as in the Old Testament, a law of fear. He again emphasizes the important fact that the whole Decalogue may be summed up in the two great commandments of love of God and of our neighbor. Augustine was the first to interpret the Decalogue in its New Testament or Christian sense and to show that it adequately expresses the Christian moral code. Cf. P. Rentschka, *Die Dekalogkatechese des hl. Augustinus. Ein Beitrag zur Geschichte des Dekalogs* (Kempten 1905) 108 f. For the thought, cf. the hymn for Pentecost in the *Breviarium Parisiense: Per quem (Spiritum Sanctum) legis amor, cordibus insitus,* | *Dat quod lex iubet exsequi.*

[272] Rom. 5. 5: *Caritas Dei diffusa est in cordibus nostris per Spiritum Sanctum, qui datus est nobis.* This is one of Augustine's favorite texts; it occurs again in the present treatise, at the close of Ch. 14.

[273] The Latin *decalogus* is a transliteration of the Greek δεκάλογος. Augustine had a fair knowledge of Greek. Cf. P. Guilloux, "Saint

Augustin savait-il le grec?", *Rev. d'hist. eccl.* 21 (1925) 79-83; H. I. Marrou, *Saint Augustin et la fin de la culture antique* (Paris 1938) 27-46; especially, B. Altaner, "Augustinus und die griechische Sprache," *Pisciculi, Franz Joseph Dölger dargeboten* (Münster i. W. 1939) 19-40.

[274] Cf. Matt. 22. 37-40.

[275] Cf. Exod. 12.

[276] Cf. 1 Cor. 5. 7: *Etenim Pascha nostrum immolatus est Christus*; cf. also the Roman Missal, Paschal Preface: *cum Pascha nostrum immolatus est Christus. Ipse enim verus est agnus*, qui abstulit peccata mundi.

[277] Cf. Acts 2.

[278] Here the Latin for Acts 2. 2 reads: factus est *subito* de caelo sonus, *quasi ferretur flatus vehemens*. The Vulgate version reads: et factus est *repente* de caelo sonus *tamquam advenientis spiritus vehementis*; the Old Latin version reads: et factus est *repente* de caelo sonus *velut advenientis spiritus violentis*. Augustine in his quotations from the Acts of the Apostles made use of St. Cyprian's version (cf. above, n. 40). This version, which Augustine quotes at length in *Acta c. Fel. Manich.*, reads: factus est *subito* de caelo sonus, *quasi ferretur flatus vehemens*, which is identical with Augustine's present quotation. F. C. Burkitt, *The Old Latin and the Itala* (Cambridge 1896) 57, observes: ". . . But what I believe has not received sufficient attention is the remarkable extant evidence tending to shew that during S. Augustine's episcopate, from about 400 A. D. onwards, the Church at Hippo read the Gospels from S. Jerome's version, though for the Acts it retained a very pure form of the Old African Latin. The evidence is as follows. In A. D. 404 a Manichee preacher named Felix appeared at Hippo, where he was arrested and brought to trial before the ecclesiastical courts. This trial is reported at length in the tract called *Acta contra Felicem Manichaeum* (or Aug. *Contra Felicem*). The statements of Felix about the coming of the Holy Spirit had been so unsatisfactory that S. Augustine determined to read to him the full Biblical account. Accordingly a codex of the Gospels was handed to him and he read from it to Felix Le. xxiv, 36-49. Having read these verses he gave back the book of the Gospels and was then handed a codex of the Acts, from which he read the whole of the first chapter and the first eleven verses of the second. What S. Augustine read out is given *in extenso* in our MSS. of Aug. *Contra Felicem*, and an examination of the two passages leads to the surprising result that the passage from S. Luke is

pure Vulgate, while the text of the Acts is that of S. Cyprian—the very oldest form of the African version known to us. . . . We cannot therefore but conclude that the codex of the Gospels handed to S. Augustine was a Vulgate codex, and the Codex of the Acts was an Old Latin Codex containing an 'African' text—in other words, that by 404 the Gospels were read at Hippo from the Vulgate, while in some other books of the Bible, such as the Acts, the unrevised Old Latin was still publicly used."

[279] The statement that the shadow of Peter raised a dead man to life is a slip on Augustine's part. Cf. Acts 5. 15, where it is stated that the sick were so placed along the streets, "that when Peter came, his shadow at the least, might overshadow any of them, and they might be delivered from their infirmities"—*et liberarentur ab infirmitatibus suis*. This last clause, which Augustine confused, is not found in the Greek text. He does not make this slip when referring to the same passage in *In Ioan. Ev. tract.* 71. 3. F. C. Burkitt, "St. Augustine's Bible and the Itala," *Jour. of Theol. Stud.* 11 (1909) 450, appositely observes: "Nor is there any reason to suppose that St. Augustine never made downright mistakes. He certainly put Barnabas instead of Silas into the prison at Philippi (in Ioan. 113), a reading for which neither the Vulgate nor the Old Latin of Acts 16, 25 is responsible. . . . It is very hard to write a book upon textual subjects without making occasional mistakes." In *Retr.* 2. 4, Augustine's excuse for synchronizing Plato and Jeremias is: *me fefellit memoria*. We know that Augustine was familiar with the apocryphal *Acts of Peter* (see his *C. Adimant.* 17. 5); in these acts, Ch. 26, 27, 28, three distinct references are made to persons raised from the dead by Peter. It is just possible, therefore, that Augustine confused the account given in the Acts of the Apostles with one of those taken from the apocryphal *Acts of Peter* (cf. M. R. James, *The Apocryphal New Testament* [Oxford 1924] 326-29).

[280] Cf. Matt. 19. 21; Luke 18. 22.

[281] Cf. Acts 4. 34.

[282] Cf. Acts 4. 32: Multitudinis autem credentium erat cor unum, et anima una; *nec quisquam eorum, quae possidebat, aliquid suum esse dicebat; sed erant illis omnia communia.* It has been objected by some scholars that Augustine's theory of property has been vitiated by the undue prominence he gives to this text. Augustine, like Ambrose, in the opinion of these scholars, believed that this text implies a permanent condemnation of private property. For a defence of Augustine against this charge of "Christian Communism," cf.

B. Roland-Gosselin, *La morale de Saint Augustin* (Paris 1925) 168-218; J. Mausbach, *Die Ethik des heiligen Augustinus* (2d ed., Freiburg i. Br. 1929) 1. 284 ff.

[283] The Jews, by dispersing the Christians, were unconsciously spreading abroad the faith. Augustine is fond of emphasizing this providential fact; cf., for example, *Serm.* 116. 6: Lapidato Stephano, passa est illa congeries persecutionem: sparsa sunt ligna, et accensus est mundus; *Serm.* 316. 4.

[284] The usual name of "Christians" in the New Testament; cf. Rom. 1. 7: *vocatis sanctis* (κλητοῖς ἁγίοις).

[285] Cf. Acts 8. 3 and 9. 1.

[286] *Praedicare*, with or without *Evangelium*, is the word regularly used by the Fathers to designate the spreading of the Christian faith.

[287] For St. Paul's account of his sufferings, cf. 2 Cor. 11. 23-27. Though formerly a persecutor, he labored hard as an Apostle: cf. 1 Cor. 15. 9.

[288] Cf. Acts 24. 17; Rom. 15. 26; 1 Cor. 16; 2 Cor. 8 and 9.

[289] Augustine frequently refers to the clergy as *milites* ("soldiers"), and to the laity as *provinciales* ("provincials"): as the *provinciales* support the soldiers who protect them, by paying taxes, so the laity must support the clergy. This comparison is borrowed from St. Paul; cf. 1 Cor. 9. 7 and 14: *Quis militat suis stipendiis umquam?* . . . *Ita et Dominus ordinavit iis, qui Evangelium annunciant, de Evangelio vivere* (cf. also 2 Cor. 11. 8). For the same comparison in St. Augustine, cf. *In Ioan. Ev. tract.* 122. 3: Satis igitur apertum est, non imperatum, sed in potestate apostolis positum, ut aliunde non viverent nisi ex Evangelio . . . et *tamquam milites Christi* stipendium debitum acciperent, *sicut a provincialibus Christi*; cf. also *Enarr. in Ps.* 90, *serm.* 1. 10; *Enarr. in Ps.* 103, *serm.* 3. 9; *Serm.* 351. 5.

[290] Cf. Acts 4. 11; Eph. 2. 20; also Ps. 117. 2 and Isa. 28. 16.

[291] Cf. Augustine, *Serm.* 252. 3; Optatus 3. 10: Nec lapidem habere angularem unus paries potest, *qui lapis est Christus duos in se suscipiens populos, unum de gentibus, alterum de Iudaeis*; also the hymn, *Urbs beata Ierusalem*, 13 f.:

> Angulare fundamentum lapis Christus missus est,
> Qui compage parietum in utroque nectitur.

To appreciate this metaphor of the corner-stone (Christ) in which are linked together as portions of the building both Jew and Gentile, we must bear in mind that it is Oriental. J. A. Robinson, *St. Paul's Epistle to the Ephesians* (2d ed., London 1914) 69, writes: "When

St. Paul speaks of Christ as the corner-stone, he uses a metaphor which appears to be wholly Oriental. The Greeks laid no stress on corner-stones. We must go to the East if we would understand at all what they mean. The corner-stones in the temple substructures . . . are not, as we might perhaps have supposed, stones so shaped as to contain a right-angle, and thus by their projecting arms to bind two walls together. . . . They are straight blocks which run up to a corner, where they are met in the angle by similar stones, the ends of which come immediately above or below them. These straight blocks are of great length, frequently measuring fifteen feet. . . . It was such a stone as this that furnished the ancient prophet with his image of the Messiah."

292 Matt. 10. 16. The sufferings of the martyrs appealed particularly to Augustine. Many of his finest sermons were delivered on their anniversaries. Note, for example, *Serm.* 309-13 in honor of St. Cyprian; *Serm.* 317-19 in honor of St. Stephen. For his solicitude for a worthy form of veneration of the martyrs, cf. J. Quasten, " 'Vetus Superstitio et Nova Religio.' The Problem of *Refrigerium* in the Ancient Church of North Africa," *Harv. Theol. Rev.* 33 (1940) 253-66.

293 Tertullian had written the celebrated words, *Apol.* 50. 13: Etiam plures efficimur, quotiens metimur a vobis: *semen est sanguis Christianorum*; cf. also Jerome, *Ep.* 27. 2: *Est sanguis martyrum seminarium ecclesiarum*; Augustine, *De civ. Dei* 22. 6: Ligabantur, includebantur, caedebantur, torquebantur, urebantur, laniabantur, trucidabantur et—multiplicabantur.

294 John 15. 2.

295 Heresy and schism were of value to the Church: 1) they gave the faithful an opportunity to practice patience and forbearance; 2) they were frequently the occasion of councils of the Church at which not only was heresy condemned but dogma was defined and explained. Cf. 1 Cor. 11. 19: *Nam oportet et haereses esse, ut et qui probati sunt manifesti fiant in vobis*; Augustine, *Conf.* 7. 19. 25: *Improbatio quippe haereticorum facit eminere, quid Ecclesia tua sentiat et quid habeat sana doctrina*; Vincent of Lerins, *Common.* 20.

296 Cf. Matt. 25. 31 ff.

297 A favorite thought of Augustine's: cf. *Conf.* 1. 6. 9: Fuine alicubi aut aliquis? Nam quis mihi dicat ista, non habeo; nec pater nec mater potuerunt nec aliorum experimentum, nec memoria mea. See 2 Mac. 7. 22.

298 It should be noted that Augustine here speaks of the various

periods of growth from infancy to old age as *aetates*, which in classical Latin is used only of ages, generations, or epochs in a general sense (as in the present treatise, 22. 39; cf. n. 249). Augustine most probably applied the term *aetates* to these periods of growth and development because he is fond of comparing the six periods of man's life (*infantia, pueritia, adolescentia, iuventus, gravitas, senectus*) to the evolution which takes place in the six epochs into which the history of the world is divided (above, nn. 249-51). Cf. *De civ. Dei* 10. 14: *Sicut autem unius hominis, ita humani generis . . . recta eruditio per quosdam articulos temporum tamquam aetatum profecit accessibus; De div. quaest.* 1. 58; *De vera rel.* 50; *De Gen. c. Man.* 1. 39.

⁹⁹ Cf. Tertullian, *Apol.* 48: Ideoque repraesentabuntur et corpora, quia neque pati quicquam potest anima sola sine stabili materia, id est carne; et quod omnino de iudicio Dei pati debent animae, non sine carne meruerunt, intra quam omnia egerunt; Minucius Felix, *Oct.* 35: Sicut ignes fulminum corpora tangunt nec absumunt, . . . ita poenale illud incendium non damnis ardentium pascitur, sed inexesa corporum laceratione nutritur.

³⁰⁰ Cf. Isa. 66. 24; Mark 9. 43; Apoc. 9. 6; 14. 11. Noteworthy are these descriptions by Augustine: *Serm.* 307. 5: Mors secunda et mors vocatur, et nemo ita moritur, potius et melius dixerim, nemo ibi vivit, in doloribus enim vivere, non est vivere; *De civ. Dei.* 19. 28: Miseria sempiterna, quae mors etiam secunda dicitur, quia nec anima ibi vivere dicenda est quae a vita Dei alienata erit, nec corpus, quod aeternis doloribus subiacebit; ac per hoc ideo durior ista secunda mors, quia finiri morte non poterit.

³⁰¹ Cf. Mark 12. 25; Luke 20. 36.

³⁰² Cf. 2 Cor. 5. 7. For Augustine's definition of *species* (" beatific vision "), cf. *De Trin.* 14. 2: Neque enim iam fides erit qua credantur quae non videntur, sed *species, qua videantur quae credebantur.* The opening lines of Tennyson's *In Memoriam* come to mind:

> Strong Son of God, immortal Love,
>   Whom we, that have not seen thy face,
>   By faith, and faith alone, embrace,
> Believing where we cannot prove.
>
> .   .   .   .
>
> We have but faith; we cannot know;
>   For knowledge is of things we see.

³⁰³ Cf. John 20. 29.

[304] Cf. the preparation for intuition described by Plotinus, *Enn.*
5. 1. 2. P. Pourrat, *Christian Spirituality* (trans. by W. M. Mitchell
and S. P. Jacques, London 1922) 1. 211, observes: " In order to arrive
at contemplation the soul requires far more moral preparation than
for the rational knowledge of God. The Neo-Platonists attached the
highest importance to this preparation. Enlightened by Christian
faith, St. Augustine also insists on it. He knows that contemplation
is entirely a spiritual phenomenon, altogether divine; the soul cannot
reach it without at the outset freeing itself from the senses and from
all that is of the body, so that it may retire within itself and receive
the divine light." Read Augustine's last conversation with Monnica
at Ostia before her death, *Conf.* 9. 10. 24.

[305] *Hostis* (" enemy ") is a common epithet of the devil in the
Fathers; cf., e. g., Ambrose, *De interp. David* 6. 28: ne *hostis* introeat.

[306] The devil is jealous of man and finds his only consolation in
trying to make him a fellow in his damnation. See Wisd. 2. 24:
Invidia autem diaboli mors introivit in orbem terrarum. See Tertullian, *Apol.* 22; Minucius Felix, *Oct.* 26. 8; Lactantius, *Inst. div.*
2. 14. 11: Solatium perditionis suae perdendis hominibus (daemones)
operantur; etc. See also Milton, *Paradise Lost* 9. 126 ff.:

> Nor hope to be myself less miserable
> By what I seek, but others to make such
> As I, though thereby worse to me redound:
> For only in destroying I find ease
> To my relentless thoughts.

[307] The Donatists are referred to who as schismatics were cut off
from the vine of the Church as dead branches. No Father of the
Church has insisted more than Augustine on the necessity of union
with the see of Peter. Cf. P. Batiffol, *Le catholicisme de S. Augustin*
(3d ed., Paris 1920) 1. 192-209, Exc. B: " La ' Cathedra Petri ' dans
la controverse antidonatiste d'Augustin."

[308] Eccli. 18. 9.

[309] On January 29, 399, the emperor Honorius issued a decree
forbidding the worship of idols and ordering the destruction of pagan
temples. As the second part of the decree had not been carried out
in Africa, the bishops sent a delegation to Rome, asking that it be
enforced. Their request was granted, and on March 19, 399, the
pagan temple in Carthage was destroyed. Many who were still
pagans at heart became Christians, but in name only. Though
obliged by law to attend church services—at which not infrequently

they showed gross disrespect—they continued to observe privately their pagan customs and practices and celebrated the *dies sollemnes paganorum*. Cf. Augustine, *De civ. Dei* 1.35; also *Serm.* 196 and 198. Read G. Boissier, *La fin du paganisme* (Paris 1891) 2. 370-72.

The word "pagan," *paganus*, originally meant "a civilian" as opposed to "a soldier"; cf. Pliny, *Ep.* 10. 18: *et milites et pagani*; also Juvenal, *Sat.* 16. 33. As the civilians (*pagani*) were less amenable to imperial influence (which from Constantine on was usually exerted in favor of Christianity) than were the military and others in the employ of the government, *paganus* gradually became synonomous with "non-Christian." This theory is held by A. Harnack (*Die Mission und Ausbreitung des Christentums* [4th ed., Leipzig 1924] 1. 430 ff.) and by T. Zahn ("Paganus," *Neue kirchl. Zeitschr.* 10 [1899] 18-43). According to the traditional explanation *paganus* is derived from *pagus*; hence its original meaning was a "rustic," "a dweller in the country." As the country districts were the last to embrace Christianity, *paganus* came to be associated with backwardness in accepting Christianity. The traditional explanation would seem to be sounder. It has been ably defended by M. J. Zeiller, *Paganus; étude de terminologie historique* (Collectanea Friburg. 17 [26], Fribourg 1917) 19; 43. For the use of the synonyms *ethnicus, gentilis*, and *paganus* in the sermons of Augustine, cf. C. Mohrmann, *Die altchristliche Sondersprache in den Sermonen des hl. Augustin* (Lat. Christ. Prim. 3, Nijmegen 1932) 110.

[810] Cf. Matt. 7. 21 f. Augustine's quotation may represent a conflation of this passage in Matthew and Luke 13. 26; or in Matt. 7. 22 he may be following a text that survives as a variant in the Greek text of this verse.

[811] Here the term *praevaricatores* is used, which originally meant advocates found guilty of collusion with the opposing counsel (cf. Cicero, *De part. orat.* 126). In ecclesiastical Latin it is applied to the sinner who is unfaithful to his obligations to God, being a stronger term than *peccator*.

[812] No one knew better than St. Augustine the power of good example. He is forever exhorting the catechumens to associate with the good; cf. *Serm.* 223. 1; 224. 1; 228. 2.

[813] Cf. Matt. 5. 43; Jer. 17. 5.

[813a] Cf. 1 Cor. 10. 13.

[814] Augustine is most probably quoting the exact words of an early liturgical formula. A profession of faith was required of all candi-

dates before their admission to the catechumenate; this profession of faith took the form of question and answer. A relic of such inter-rogatory liturgical formulae is seen in the questions still put to the one to be baptized or, in the case of an infant, to the sponsors. Cf. the Roman Ritual, *Ordo Baptismi*:

> Quid petis ab Ecclesia Dei? Fidem.
> Fides quid tibi praestat? Vitam aeternam. . . .
> Credis in deum Patrem Omnipotentem, Creatorem
>   caeli et terrae? Credo. . . .

On the liturgical and disciplinary questions put to candidates for baptism in the early Church, cf. T. Schermann, *Die allgemeine Kirchenordnung des 2. Jahrhunderts* (Stud. z. Gesch. u. Kult. d. Altert., Ergänzungsb. 3. 1, Paderborn 1914) 61-64.

[315] The Benedictine editors conjecture *salis* ("salt") for *sane*, which conjecture I have followed in my translation. From the context it is abundantly clear that the reference is solely to the administering of salt to the catechumen and not to the other two initiatory rites which consisted in the insufflation with a formulary of exorcism and the signing with the Cross on the forehead (cf. Ch. 8 and n. 87). When, for instance, in *Conf.* 8. 2. 4, he refers to the initiatory rites, he uses the plural: *primis instructionis sacramentis*; if therefore he uses the singular here, it is because he is referring to one particular ceremony.

The salt was exorcised before being administered to the cate-chumen. For this, cf. the Roman Ritual, *Ordo Baptismi: Exorcizo te, creatura salis in nomine Dei Patris Omnipotentis.* The admin-istration of salt is regularly referred to as a *sacramentum*: cf. the formula in the Gelasian Sacramentary: *ut haec creatura salis* in nomine Trinitatis *efficiatur salutare sacramentum* ad effugandum diabolum; also *Concilium Carthaginiense* 3. 5 (Mansi 3. 919): Item placuit ut etiam per sollemnissimos paschales dies *sacramentum* catechumenis non detur nisi solitum *sal.*

[316] Salt is used for preserving, purifying, cleansing; hence its symbolical meaning. Cf. Matt. 5. 13: *Vos estis sal terrae. Quod si sal evanuerit, in quo salietur?* Note also Augustine, *Conf.* 1. 11. 17: *et signabar iam signo Crucis et condiebar eius sale.* For other refer-ences, cf. F. J. Dölger, *Der Exorzismus im altchristlichen Taufritual* (Stud. z. Gesch. u. Kult. d. Altert. 3. 1-2, Paderborn 1909).

[317] That is, love of God and love of neighbor (Matt. 12. 30 f.).

[318] Cf. Rom. 2. 4.

[319] The wise catechist will study his audience to find out what their mental capacity is, and what their interests are, so that he may be able to accommodate his instructions accordingly.

[320] Cf. 1 John 2. 16 f.

[321] God in His mercy wills to save all men unless, being their own worst enemies (and this is the necessary restriction to God's will to save men), they will to be damned. Cf. 1 Tim. 2. 4: *Omnes homines vult salvos fieri, et ad agnitionem veritatis venire.* This passage from the *De cat. rud.* is frequently cited in demonstrating God's antecedent will to save men. The *locus classicus* for Augustine's teaching on this point is *De spir. et litt.* 58: *Vult autem Deus omnes homines salvos fieri et in agnitionem veritatis venire, non sic tamen ut eis adimet liberum arbitrium quo vel bene vel male utentes iustissime iudicentur.*

[322] Cf. 1 John 4. 9 and John 1. 3.

[323] Christ by becoming man did not cease to be God. For the thought, cf. Augustine, *Serm.* 184. 1: *in homine ad nos venisse, et a Patre non recessisse; Ep.* 170. 9: *homo assumtus est a Deo, non in homine consumtus est Deus*; etc. Cf. the Eucharistic hymn of St. Thomas Aquinas:

> *Verbum supernum prodiens,*
> *Nec Patris linquens dexteram.*

Almost three hundred years before Augustine, Ignatius of Antioch had written, *Magn.* 7. 2 (trans. by J. A. Kleist, *ACW* 1. 71): ". . . who came forth from one Father and yet remained with, and returned to, one."

[324] Cf. Rom. 5. 12.

[325] Cf. 1 Tim. 2. 14.

[326] This section (53) on the triumph and progress of Christianity is frequently quoted. Cf. Tertullian's famous description to the pagan Roman governors of the growth of the Christian religion in *Apol.* 37: *Hesterni sumus, et vestra omnia implevimus—urbes, insulas, castella, municipia.* Cf. also Augustine, *De ver. rel.* 4. 6.

[327] The simile of the Church as a ship is found throughout the Greek and Latin Fathers. The earliest example may be seen in Ignatius of Antioch, *Pol.* 2. 3 (cf. J. B. Lightfoot's notes: *The Apostolic Fathers, Part II: S. Ignatius, S. Polycarp* [2d ed., London 1889] 2. 340 f.).

[328] Cf. Gen. 12. 2 f.

[329] Here the word *passiones* is used. The term *passio*, even without a qualifying possessive, was used originally of Christ's Passion (cf.

Acts I. 3: quibus et praebuit seipsum vivum post *passionem* suam); later on its use (singular and plural) was extended to the sufferings and death of the martyrs and then, by a very natural development, to the narrative of these sufferings (e. g., *Passio sanctarum Perpetuae et Felicitatis*) .

[330] Cf. Matt. 24. 5.

[331] That is, bad Catholics and schismatics. The metaphor is derived from Matt. 3. 12. Augustine usually makes a distinction in the use of *paleae* ("chaff") and *zizania* ("cockle," "tares," "weeds"; cf. Matt. 13. 25 ff.): *paleae* referring to bad Catholics, *zizania*, to heretics; cf., for instance, *Quaest. sept. in Ev. Matth.* 11. 1.

[332] Earlier, in Ch. 25. 46, Augustine had written *Numquid ergo difficile est Deo . . . reddere istam quantitatem corporis tui sicut erat, qui eam facere potuit sicut non erat?* The argument that it is easier for God to restore man's body on the last day than it was to create him originally out of nothing is a commonplace among the apologists. Cf. Minucius Felix, *Oct.* 34. 9: Porro *difficilius est id quod non sit incipere quam id quod fuerit iterare*; Tertullian, *Apol.* 48. 6; Lactantius, *Inst. div.* 7. 23. 5. In the present passage Augustine is even more explicit about the identity of the body at resurrection. In the next world the body, in which we have done good or evil in this life, will furnish the "material" for our reward or punishment. On this, cf. also Tertullian, *Apol.* 48; *De res. carn.* 14.

[333] Cf. Luke 20. 36; also Matt. 22. 30 and Mark 12. 25.

[334] Cf. 1 Peter 5. 8.

[335] The candidate is to regard the *perfectiones mixtae*—the attributes common to God and man—not as they are found in man, limited and imperfect, but as they are found in God, that is, in their highest perfection.

[336] Cf. 1 Tim. 2. 5: Unus enim Deus, *unus et mediator Dei et hominum homo Christus Iesus.*

[337] *Homines ergo bonos imitare, malos tolera, omnes ama*: this epigrammatic rule, in which Augustine summarizes the Christian's obligations towards his neighbor, is frequently quoted.

[338] Matt. 22. 40.

[339] Christian writers, when speaking of our spiritual struggles, frequently make use of military terms. For an interesting discussion of this subject, cf. A. Harnack, *Militia Christi: die christliche Religion und der Soldatenstand in den ersten drei Jahrhunderten* (Leipzig 1905). See also for Tertullian, St. W. J. Teeuwen, *Sprachlicher Bedeutungswandel bei Tertullian* (Stud. z. Gesch. u. Kult. d. Altert.

14. 1, Paderborn 1926) 101-120: "Aus der Soldatensprache."
Martyrdom especially is seen in all the panoply of warfare: cf.
E. L. Hummel, *The Concept of Martyrdom according to St. Cyprian
of Carthage* (Stud. in Christ. Ant. 9, Washington 1946) 56-90:
"Martyrdom as a Spiritual Warfare: a Contest with the Devil."

[340] Augustine improves every opportunity of mentioning the two
great Christian virtues, upon which he has insisted so much throughout this treatise: charity and humility.

[341] Cf. 1 Cor. 10. 13. On the value of temptation in the spiritual
life, read Augustine, *Enarr. in Ps.* 60. 3: Vita nostra in hac peregri-
natione non potest esse sine tentatione: quia provectus noster per
tentationem nostram fit, nec sibi quisque innotescit nisi tentatus, nec
potest coronari nisi vicerit, nec potest vincere nisi certaverit, nec
potest certare nisi inimicum et tentationes habuerit.

INDEX

Abraham, 60, 62, 70, 84, 130
Abt, A., 107
accedentes, 3, 4
acroamatic, method of catechizing, 116 f.
actors, 54, 81, 122
Acts of the Apostles, 18, 100
Acts of Peter 26, 27, 28: 140
Adam, 70, 84, 103, 125
Adeodatus, 93
adolescentia, 143
adulterers, 80
advena, 118
advent, of a king to a city, 98
aequalis gloria, 130
aetates, of history, 136; of man's growth, 143
Africa, 7, 93, 105, 106, 118, 144
Africans, nature of, 114; vices of, 122
ἀγάπη, spiritual love, 101
Albicerius, diviner, 107
Alcuin, 9
d'Alès, A., 9, 99, 108
Alexander the Great, 135
Alexandria, 3, 120
allegory, 33, 113, 123, 132, 136
Allgeier, A., 92, 103
Altaner, B., 139
Ambrose, St., and Clement of Rome, 105; use of allegorism, 113; St. Augustine attracted by, 116; 7, 132, 140
  Apol. David 1.2: 97; *De Abraham*: 4; *De fuga saec.* 20:

104; *De Iacob* 1. 5. 17: 124; *De interp. David* 6. 28: 144; *De myst.*: 4; *De off.* 3. 18. 103: 124; *De patr.* 4. 24: 124; *De Spir. Sanc.* 3. 2. 13: 132; *Ep.* 33: 94; *Exp. in Ps.* 118, *serm.* 15. 9: 132; *serm.* 18. 26: 91; *Exp. Ev. sec. Lucam* 5. 75: 101; 7. 7: 124; *Hex.* 1. 6: 116
Ammianus Marcellinus 14. 6. 4: 124
amor, 101
amplification, in rhetoric, 137
angelic incorruption, 86
angels, have free will, 59; ruled by the Word of God, 66; rest in Christ; the fallen, 66, 126; 45, 59, 78, 86, 129
anger, 15 f.
anniversaries, of martyrs, 142
anthropomorphism, in conception of God, 132; in Scripture, 102
Antiochus Epiphanes, 135
antistes, 113
antithesis, Augustine's use of, 137
apathy, of the catechized, 42-45
Apocalypse, 96
apologists, 129, 148
Apostles, descent of Holy Ghost upon, 138
apparere, 97, 98
applause, 114
Apuleius, *Apol.* 13. 416: 121
Aquila, 99